D0723212

10/23

BAGRATION 1944

BAGRATION 1944

THE DESTRUCTION OF ARMY GROUP CENTRE

STEVEN J ZALOGA

OPPOSITE

Two of the Red Army's finest commanders, Marshals Konstantin Rokossovskiy (left) and Georgi Zhukov (right). Rokossovskiy commanded the 1st Ukrainian Front during Operation Bagration, while Zhukov served as the STAVKA representative to the two southern fronts. (Sovfoto)

First published in Great Britain in 1996 by
Osprey, a division of Reed Consumer Books
Limited, Michelin House, 81 Fulham Road,
London SW3 6RB and Auckland, Melbourne,
Singapore and Toronto

© Copyright 1996
Reed International Books Ltd.
Reprinted 1997 (twice)

All rights reserved. Apart from any fair
dealing for the purpose of private study,
research, criticism or review, as permitted
under the Copyright, Designs and Patents Act,
1988, no part of this publication may be
reproduced, stored in a retrieval system, or
transmitted in any form or by any means
electronic, electrical, chemical, mechanical,
optical, photocopying, recording or otherwise,
without the prior written permission of the
copyright owner. Enquiries should be
addressed to the Publishers.

ISBN 1 85532 478 4

Military Editor: Lee Johnson.

Designed by Paul Kime.

Colour bird's eye view illustrations
by Peter Harper.

Cartography by Micromap.
Wargaming *Operation Bagration*
by Ian Drury.

Filmset in Great Britain.
Printed through World Print Ltd.,
Hong Kong

KEY TO MILITARY SYMBOLS

Army Group	xxxxx	Regiment	iii	Artillery	•
Army	xxxx	Battalion	ii	Armour	◯
Corps	xxx	Company	i	Motorized	⊠
Division	xx	Infantry		Airborne	
Brigade	x	Cavalry		Special Forces	

If you would like to receive more information about
Osprey Military books, The Osprey Messenger is a
regular newsletter which contains articles, new title
information and special offers. To join please write to:

**Osprey Military Messenger,
PO Box 443,
Peterborough PE2 6LA**

CONTENTS

STRATEGIC SITUATION ON THE EASTERN FRONT, 23 JUNE 1944

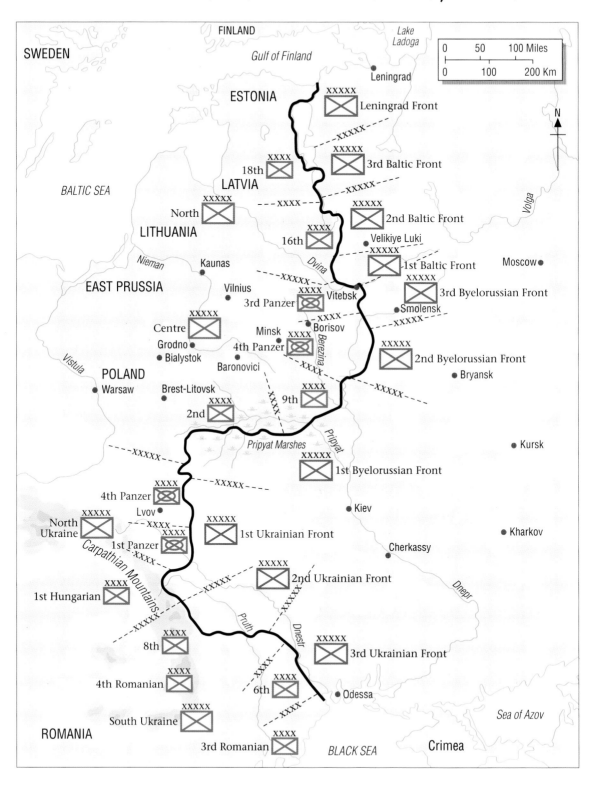

ORIGINS
OF THE BATTLE

A Soviet ML-20 152mm gun-howitzer crew loads its weapon. During the initial artillery barrage opening Operation Bagration the average weapon expended about two units of fire during the first hours, equivalent for this weapon to about 6 tons of projectiles. (Sovfoto)

On 22 June 1944, three years to the day after Germany's 1941 invasion of the Soviet Union, the Red Army launched a massive offensive in Byelorussia. Codenamed 'Operation Bagration', this campaign climaxed five weeks later with the Red Army at the gates of Warsaw. In many respects Operation Bagration was the 1941 Operation Barbarossa invasion in reverse, fought over many of the same battlefields. The Wehrmacht's Army Group Centre was routed, a total of 17 Wehrmacht divisions were utterly destroyed, and over 50 other German divisions were shattered. It was the most calamitous defeat of the German armed forces in World War II, costing the Wehrmacht more men and materiel than the cataclysm at Stalingrad 16 months earlier. It was all the more catastrophic when the Anglo-American forces in Normandy inflicted a similar blow in August 1944 by trapping the Wehrmacht forces in the Falaise pocket in France. Although known to historians of the Eastern Front, this important campaign is little appreciated in the West, overshadowed by the Normandy campaign.

The German Wehrmacht had managed to maintain the strategic initiative on the Eastern Front until the summer of 1943, when Operation Citadel, its Kursk-Orel offensive, was decisively repulsed. Following this defeat, the Red Army began a series of offensive operations that were most successful in Ukraine. On 3 August they launched Operation Rumyantsev, and by the end of August the industrial city of Kharkov in eastern Ukraine had been liberated. In the ensuing fighting, in the early autumn of 1943, the Red Army aimed for the Dnepr river. The Ukraine's vast steppes provided little natural defensive advantage for the Germans, and the Dnepr river formed the only major natural obstacle. By mid-October the Red Army had reached the Dnepr and even managed to secure small footholds on its western banks. Soviet operations were not confined to this sector alone, further south they had cut off German and Romanian forces on the Crimean peninsula during their Black Sea offensive in September.

The Germans' vigorous defence of the Dnepr river line led the STAVKA (the Soviet high command) to attempt an outflanking move further north. Along the Byelorussian-Ukrainian border the Red Army secured a substantial penetration westward into the Pripyat marshes area. Striking southward from these newly gained positions in mid-November, the offensive

unhinged the Dnepr river line, and Kiev was liberated in December 1943. The Red Army then began an arduous push westward along the southern reaches of the Pripyat marshes, approaching the former (1939) Soviet borders by the end of winter. Before Christmas 1943 they renewed their offensives against the Dnepr river line. Striking south-west from Kiev, the Red Army's 1st Ukrainian Front pushed the Wehrmacht back towards the Bug river. In late January the 2nd Ukrainian Front trapped a substantial German force in the Korsun-Shevchenkovskiy pocket, but Generalfeldmarschall Erich von Manstein employed the 3rd Panzer Corps to rupture the Soviet cordon and relieve the pocket. By the middle of February about 30,000 troops had been pulled out, but German losses were substantial. The Soviet facility with armoured formations, even under harsh winter conditions, was extremely alarming to veteran German commanders; no previous Soviet winter offensives had been so boldly executed.

The growing strength of the Red Army meant that they could carry out operations in other areas as well. In the late autumn of 1943 an offensive was launched against Army Group North and Army Group Centre in northern Russia. In October they struck near Nevel, and managed to push the German defensive line from western Russia into the Baltic republics and Byelorussia. The bitter fighting in this sector lasted well into December, and largely determined the frontlines for the ensuing battle for Byelorussia, in the summer of 1944. The situation was equally bleak for the Germans in the north. After two years of siege, the Red Army managed to end the

The bitter winter fighting in January 1944 set the battle lines for the summer 1944 confrontation on the Eastern Front. Here PzKpfw IV tanks of the 48 Panzer Corps pass through Zhitomir during the savage fighting against Rybalko's 3rd Guards Tank Army. (Janusz Magnuski)

The Germany Army's exploitation of careless Russian radio transmissions in World War I had convinced the Red Army to maintain strict radio security. During the planning for Operation Bagration, radio transmission was kept to a minimum. Here a colonel of a Guards artillery regiment receives instructions over a secure land-line telephone while his female wireless operator decodes an encrypted radio transmission. (Sovfoto)

blockade of Leningrad and push Army Group North back over 100km to the west side of Lake Peipus.

The culmination of Red Army operations in the autumn of 1943 and early winter 1944 was yet another offensive, this time against Army Group South in Ukraine. On 4 March 1944 the 1st, 2nd and 3rd Ukrainian fronts began a massive attack, hoping to push the Germans out of Ukraine before the spring rains arrived. By the end of March they had pushed westward and southward, nearing the pre-war borders with Poland and Romania; there the offensive was halted. The German and Romanian forces trapped on the Crimean peninsula were finally overcome by mid-May 1944. Further operations in Ukraine and Byelorussia in the late spring were out of the question, due to the general exhaustion of the Red Army and the spring mud. However, there was no doubt among German commanders that their respite would be brief.

The failure of the German army to resist the Red Army advances in late 1943 and early 1944 led to sweeping personnel changes in the upper leadership of the Wehrmacht and a rigid centralisation of command under Hitler, who blamed the senior generals for the defeats, especially the more outspoken ones who questioned his military judgement. As a result, Hitler came to be surrounded increasingly by the more sycophantic generals, who would tolerate his bullying and acquiesce to his increasingly unrealistic schemes. Symptomatic of this trend was Hitler's relief of Generalfeldmarschall Erich von Manstein, widely regarded as the most brilliant of the

German commanders on the Eastern Front. Von Manstein's skilful leadership had been instrumental in blunting the Soviet offensives in Ukraine, but his realistic appraisals of Germany's options in the East were branded by Hitler as defeatist.

During the spring of 1944 both sides prepared for a summer campaign. The Germans knew that once the spring mud dried, the Red Army would be back on the offensive. The question was where? There were several plausible alternatives. The winter-spring 1943/44 campaign strongly suggested that the offensive would come again in Ukraine. There were many sound reasons for this. To begin with, the terrain favoured such an option: Ukraine marked the beginning of the great European steppe, with relatively unobstructed terrain suitable for mechanised operations. Moving west out of Ukraine, the Soviets would have several strategic possibilities; a bold stroke north to the Baltic could cut off Army Group Centre in the Byelorussian 'Balcony' as well as Army Group North along the Baltic coast. Even if such a bold approach was not taken, an assault from northern Ukraine would lead the Red Army into the Polish plains, a direct route to Berlin; by striking southward, the Red Army could spill into Romania and seize the oil fields that were fuelling the German war effort. The Germans were well aware that their Romanian and Hungarian allies were unhappy and might switch sides at any moment. The loss of Romania would eventually mean the collapse of the German war economy.

This last option seemed less attractive for the Soviets. An attack from southern Ukraine directly into Romania was certainly possible, but such an assault would be very vulnerable to a counterblow from the heavy concentration of German forces in Army Group North Ukraine. Furthermore, both Hitler and the OKH (the German high command) concurred that the main Soviet objective would be Germany, and the indirect approach south past the Carpathian Mountains was not plausible. Certainly, Romania, Hungary and the Balkans would feature in Soviet plans, but as secondary theatres of operation.

An attack on Army Group North in the Baltic was considered quite likely, but of less strategic consequence. The terrain in the Baltic favoured the defender, and a direct assault on German forces in the region would be costly and have little potential for a dramatic advance. Byelorussia was also dismissed by the German OKH high command. The Germans certainly appreciated that a defeat of Army Group Centre would open the door to the Polish plains by the northern route over the Pripyat marshes, but the terrain in Byelorussia was less suitable for advance than in Ukraine; wooded and often swampy. The road network was poor, which combined with the terrain conditions meant that supply for a sustained Soviet offensive would be difficult logistically. Furthermore, the Germans were far more confident they could hold this theatre. The Red Army had tried repeatedly to overwhelm Army Group Centre since January 1942, but in every case had either been rebuffed or gained ground at appalling cost. The autumn 1943 offensive, Operation Suvorov's 'battle for the highways', was a good example of the tenacity of German defence in this sector and the continuing difficulty the Red Army experienced operating in the Moscow-Minsk-Warsaw strategic direction.

The staff of a Soviet Guards regiment prepares final plans during the preparations for Operation Bagration. By 1944 Red Army officers were much younger than in the pre-war army, but also much more experienced. (Sovfoto)

There was a another, subconscious, reason for the German conviction that the Red Army would attack in Ukraine. Hitler, in particular, was susceptible to wishful thinking, especially when faced with the likelihood that the Anglo-American forces would launch a cross-Channel invasion of France in the summer of 1944. A Soviet offensive out of Ukraine suggested worrisome possibilities, but it also presented a hope for dramatic Soviet reversals. Should the Soviets strike northward from Ukraine, through Poland to the Baltic, in an attempt to cut off both Army Group North and Army Group Centre, this would create conditions for a German counter-stroke by Army Group Centre and Army Group North Ukraine that could cut off a large part of the Red Army and destroy it in a great encirclement battle reminiscent of the victories of 1941/42. At this stage of the war the best the Germans could hope for would be a careless Soviet operation offering opportunities for the German defenders. An attack emanating out of northern Ukraine offered the best possibility for a dramatic reversal. These factors helped convince both Hitler and the OKH that the Soviet 1944 summer offensive would come in northern Ukraine.

As Germany prepared for this offensive, events in the West were also influencing Germany's capabilities. The expected summer Allied invasion of France had had dramatic consequences in terms of draining units out of the East. By June 1944 seven of the precious Panzer divisions were committed to France, and additional units were held back from the Eastern

Prior to Operation Bagration, most officers made a personal reconnaissance of the area where their units would attack. Here colonels Shchekal and Lukashevskiy of an unidentified Guards division make a forward survey while their Lend-Lease jeep waits in the background. (Sovfoto)

Front so they could be moved either east or west as the circumstance demanded. In the summer of 1943 about 80 per cent of German tank strength had been concentrated in the East; in 1944 this proportion was only a little more than half. Hitler was convinced of the need to defeat the Allied invasion decisively, as at Dieppe two years previously, so that Germany could then reconcentrate its might against the Soviet onslaught. Since November 1943 the Western Front had been given priority for reinforcement.

Even before the invasion of France, war was already being waged by the Anglo-American forces. The strategic bombing campaign continued to weaken German defensive capabilities. In the late spring of 1944 bomber attacks had knocked out 40 per cent of Romanian oil production and 90 per cent of German synthetic oil production. German fuel reserves were substantial, but these losses forced the Wehrmacht to curb training and to rely more heavily on rail and other means to move its armour and supplies. The continual weakening of Germany's military industrial base began to sap the strength of the Wehrmacht, but the impact would not be decisive until later that year.

The most direct consequence of the Anglo-American air campaign to the forces in the East was its impact on the Luftwaffe. German anti-aircraft artillery and related ammunition represented about a quarter of German artillery and munitions output by 1944, due to the demands of Reich defence. This had a direct impact on the ability of the industry to supply the artillery demands of the German army. As the tempo of Anglo-American strategic air attacks intensified, a larger and larger proportion of tactical aircraft were withdrawn from the Eastern Front for Reich defence. Furthermore, the Reich defence campaign was horribly costly in men and machines, especially with the advent of American escort fighters. In April and May 1944 alone the Reich fighter defence force lost the equivalent of 100 per cent of its aircraft strength and 40 per cent of its pilots in bruising encounters with the US Army Air Force. This enormous drain on resources caused by the bomber campaign meant that the Eastern Front was denuded of fighter aircraft and that air superiority would be conceded to the Red Air Force even before the summer 1944 campaign began.

THE OPPOSING COMMANDERS

The war on the Eastern Front pitted two totalitarian states against each other. Both dictators, Adolf Hitler and Iosef Stalin, played a far more critical role in tactical decision making than democratic leaders such as Roosevelt and Churchill. Psychologically the conduct of the early Eastern Front campaigns in 1941/42 had opposite effects on the two leaders, and of the two dictators, Hitler's command style had the most pernicious effect on the outcome of the Byelorussian campaign.

ADOLF HITLER

Hitler's bold gambles from 1938 to 1941 had resulted in a string of remarkable German military victories. Much of the German military leadership had been sceptical of Hitler's plans, and these early victories convinced Hitler of his genius for war, as well as creating in him a visceral disdain for the judgements of the senior German military leadership. Hitler became

The scourge of the Wehrmacht were the Soviet partisans. The partisan formations in Byelorussia were made up from Red Army soldiers who had escaped capture in the 1941 invasion, as well as young men who volunteered rather than face forced labour in Germany. Weapons came from arms abandoned in 1941 or flown in by Soviet airdrops. (Sovfoto)

The Soviet high command expected artillery to be the arm of decision in the opening phase of Operation Bagration, leading to the heaviest concentration of weapons ever seen on the Eastern Front. Here ML-20 152mm gun-howitzers of the 1st Baltic Front prepare to open fire during the preparatory bombardment. (Sovfoto)

convinced that any victory was due to his brilliance, and any defeat to the incompetence of the generals. He removed officers who questioned his judgements, and gradually became surrounded by sycophants, who would support his increasingly deluded view of the strategic situation. Hitler was a skilled amateur at military planning. His military vision had been shaped by his distinguished service as a young infantryman in World War I. Like many Germans of his generation, he was convinced that Germany could have won that war, if only it had had the will to resist. He saw himself as the embodiment of that will, and acted ruthlessly against any German commander who did not show a similar enthusiasm for 'resistance to the death'.

Hitler's strategic judgement of the Soviet Union in 1944 was that it was teetering on the edge of collapse, and would collapse, as it had in 1917, if Germany simply held on long enough. During a staff conference in 1944 he rebuked the General Staff, saying, 'Unlike the Greek gods, the Russians do not become stronger every time they fall!' He was unwilling to believe that Soviet military strength was increasing rather than weakening, since this would have undermined his confidence in the ultimate victory of Germany. As evidence continued to mount of Germany's growing weakness in the face of the two-front onslaught, Hitler continued to retreat into a world of unreality, pinning his hopes on wonder-weapons and enemy blunders.

As Germany was forced onto the strategic defensive in 1944, Hitler adamantly refused to give up an inch of territory, even when a tactical retreat would have placed German troops in better defensive positions. For Hitler, tactical retreats were signs of defeatism and a lack of will to overcome the Soviets, and woe be to any German general accused of defeatism. Symptomatic of this outlook was his 1944 instructions to German commanders on the Eastern Front to prepare major cities as Feste Platze (strongpoints). These would be the centres of resistance if the Soviets did break through the German defences, and their garrisons were expected to fight to the last man. The immediate effect of this outlook was Hitler's insistence on personal authorisation of tactical retreats, even minor ones; the Wehrmacht lost its tactical flexibility, which made it more vulnerable to the Red Army.

IOSEF STALIN

Stalin's experiences early in the war had been the opposite of Hitler's. The debacle in Finland in 1940 was humiliating enough, but Hilter's betrayal of the 1939 German-Soviet pact along with the 1941 Wehrmacht invasion had shattered Stalin's confidence in his own strategic judgements. Stalin's confidence returned after the winter of 1941-42, when the German offensive was halted in the suburbs of Moscow, but his inept plans in the summer of 1942 in Ukraine had led to another painful Soviet disaster and permitted the German army to race to Stalingrad and the Caucasus. As a consequence of these cataclysms, Stalin became less dismissive of the professional advice of the STAVKA high command, and of his more successful generals, especially Georgi Zhukov and Aleksandr Vasilevskiy. While all final military decisions rested ultimately with Stalin, his distorting influence on military planning lessened after 1942. Indeed, the growing success of the Red Army after the summer of 1943 increased his confidence in the STAVKA. He continued to impose his will on the generals, but in 1944 he proved far more willing to listen to their advice; he was very cautious not to let any single Soviet general, even Zhukov, play too decisive a role in strategic decision making, but by 1944 the STAVKA high command was given a far freer hand in the tactical conduct of the war than their German OKH counterpart.

GERMAN COMMAND STRUCTURE

The critical German field commanders during the 1944 Eastern Front campaign were the army group commanders. The army groups consisted of several corps which in turn consisted of several divisions. In the late spring of 1944 there were four army groups: North, Centre, North Ukraine and South Ukraine, commanded in June 1944 by Generaloberst Georg Lindemann, Generalfeldmarschall Ernst Busch, Generalfeldmarschall Walter Model and Generalfeldmarschall Ferdinand Schoener respectively. The two commanders most directly involved in the conduct of the summer 1944 campaign were Busch and Model.

GENERALFELDMARSCHALL WALTER MODEL

Generalfeldmarschall Walter Model had taken over command of Army Group North Ukraine in March 1944, after Hitler relieved von Manstein. Model was not typical of senior German commanders, having descended from a line of Lutheran schoolmasters rather than the Prussian aristocracy. He had won the Iron Cross for bravery as a young infantry lieutenant in

Hitler dubbed Walter Model 'my favourite field marshal'. Intended to command Army Group North Ukraine during the anticipated summer offensive, Model was shifted to Army Group Centre due to Busch's failures. (Military History Institute, US Army War College)

1915. Battle-wounds had led to his appointment to a junior position on the General Staff, and his superb service record had led to his retention in the trim Reichsheer of the inter-war years. He was not popular among fellow officers due to his lack of tact, but he was ambitious, impatient and talented. Like many staff officers, Model shunned direct involvement in politics, but his radically conservative viewpoints and antipathy towards Weimar democracy made him very comfortable with the Nazi Party.

Model's first major command in World War II was the 3rd Panzer Division, which he led from November 1940. He was admired by his men and despised by his staff officers. He bullied and cajoled his staff, but his dynamic leadership gained him grudging admiration, especially from the troops. His superb leadership of the 3rd Panzer Division in 1941, during the invasion of Russia, led to quick advancement, first to the 41st Panzer Corps, then, during the Moscow fighting in January 1942, to the command of the 9th Army. He was confident and brash, even with Hitler, who preferred him over the traditional Prussian aristocrats on the OKH staff. Hitler would tolerate a certain amount of impertinence from Model, who on more than one occasion successfully challenged Hitler's military judgement. After one argument in 1942 Hitler remarked about Model, 'Did you see that eye? I trust that man to do it. But I wouldn't want to serve under him!' Model was appointed to command Army Group North in January 1944, and in March 1944 became the Wehrmacht's youngest field marshal when he was assigned to the key position of leading Army Group North Ukraine. This appointment was the supreme sign of Hitler's favour, not only because he had replaced the legendary Erich von Manstein, but because the German OKH had already concluded that Army Group North Ukraine would bear the brunt of the Soviet 1944 summer offensive. Events dictated, however, that Generalfeldmarschall Model would command the defence against the Soviet summer offensive not as commander of Army Group North Ukraine, but as the commander of Army Group Centre.

GENERALFELDMARSCHALL ERNST BUSCH

If Model represented the more dynamic side of German combat leadership, Generalfeldmarschall Ernst Busch represented a more traditional style. Like Model, Busch had distinguished himself as a young infantry officer in World War I, receiving the Pour Le Merite for bravery. His gradual rise through the ranks of the inter-war army had been due more to his political skills than his military virtues, and he was a particularly ardent supporter of the Nazi Party. During the controversy over German actions in Czechoslovakia, Busch was one of only two generals on the General Staff to urge 'unconditional obedience' to the Fuhrer. He had commanded the 8th Corps in the 1939 Polish campaign, and had been elevated to the command of the 16th Army during the 1940 battle for France. During Operation Barbarossa, in 1941, he had remained in command of the 16th Army, which took part in the advance on Leningrad. The 16th Army saw little of the dramatic action occurring elsewhere on the Eastern Front in 1942-43, laying siege to Leningrad for over two years. Busch earned a reputation for competence, though the static nature of the Leningrad Front did not pose the types of challenges faced by more dynamic commanders like Model or von Manstein, who had been involved in many battles of manoeuvre. On 28 October 1943, following a car accident which severely injured Generalfeldmarschall Gunter von Kluge, Busch was appointed to command Army Group Centre. He was viewed by the OKH as a capable, if perhaps unexceptional, commander who was favoured by Hitler due to his unquestionable loyalty and his reluctance to query orders. In the event, it was expected that Army Group Centre would merely conduct a holding operation in the summer, while the brunt of the fighting would fall on the more dynamic Model.

Field marshal Ernst Busch, though a competent army commander during the Leningrad campaign, proved to be out of his depth as commander of Army Group Centre in the disastrous summer 1944 campaign. (Military History Institute, US Army War College)

SOVIET COMMAND STRUCTURE

The Red Army's command structure for the Byelorussian campaign was somewhat more complicated than the German if for no other reason than the sheer size of the forces arrayed in Byelorussia. The closest counterpart to the German Army Group commanders were the Soviet Front commanders. There were four fronts opposite Army Group Centre in June 1944: 1st Baltic Front (General of the Army Ivan Kh. Bagramyan); 3rd Byelorussian Front (General Colonel Ivan D. Chernyakovskiy); 2nd Byelorussian Front (General Colonel Georgi F. Zakharov); and 1st Byelorussian Front (General of the Army Konstantin K. Rokossovskiy).

GENERAL OF THE ARMY IVAN BAGRAMYAN

General Ivan Bagramyan stood out from the other commanders because he was Armenian. His early career had been unexceptional, and he was still a colonel in 1941, involved mostly in staff work. The heavy casualties of 1941-42 ensured a rapid rise for any competent officer, and Bagramyan was appointed general lieutenant in 1942, in a staff position under Marshal

General of the Army Ivan Bagramyan was a little-known staff colonel at the beginning of the war, but quickly rose to the command of armies and fronts due to his facility with the new mechanised formations. He commanded the 1st Baltic Front during Operation Bagration. (Sovfoto)

Timoshenko. Bagramyan proved to be so capable a staff officer that, though he had never led a division, he was put in command of the 16th Army of the Western Front. Under his leadership, the 16th Army had distinguished itself in the Rzhev fighting in 1942, and its exceptional performance in the February 1943 Bryansk offensive prompted Stalin to redesignate it as the 11th Guards Army (a formation that will figure prominently in this book). The successful offensive operations of the 11th Guards Army during the Kursk battle, in 1943, led to Bagramyan's promotion to general colonel, and in November 1943 he was given command of the 1st Baltic Front. He was one of the few non-Slavs to command a Soviet front in World War II, and one of the few non-generals of 1941 to rise to such a position.

GENERAL COLONEL IVAN D. CHERNYAKOVSKIY

Ivan Chernyakovskiy was the only other Soviet officer who had not been a general in 1941 to command a front in World War II. Chernyakovskiy was the youngest of the front commanders in 1944, only 38 years old. A tank officer, he had commanded the 28th Tank Division at the outbreak of the war, fighting against the 1st Panzer Division in the summer of 1941 in the Baltic region. After the heavy losses of tanks suffered in the 1941 campaign, his unit was reformed as the 241st Rifle Division, which he commanded till June 1942. With the rebuilding of the tank forces in the summer of 1942 Chernyakovskiy was selected as one of the new tank corps commanders: he helped to organise the 18th Tank Corps prior to its commitment to the Stalingrad battles. In July 1942 his meteoric rise placed him in command of the 60th Army, which he led in the fighting at Kursk, the Desna and Dnepr river crossings, the liberation of Kiev in 1943 and the fighting in Ukraine in early 1944. He was placed in command of the Western Front (later the 3rd Byelorussian Front) in April 1944. Chernyakovskiy was held in high regard by the STAVKA, this is evident from the important role assigned to Chernyakovskiy's front in the ensuing Operation Bagration. He was killed in action in February 1945, during the fighting in the Baltic.

GENERAL COLONEL GEORGI F. ZAKHAROV

General Colonel Zakharov was the most controversial of the four front commanders involved in Operation Bagration. At the outbreak of the war, in 1941, Zakharov was a general major heading the staff of the 22nd Army. He held a series of staff positions and assistant front commander slots in 1942-43, mainly in the south, including Stalingrad. He commanded the 51st Army in February 1943 and the 2nd Guards Army in July 1943. During Operation Bagration the 2nd Byelorussian Front was supposed to be commanded by Gen. I.Y. Petrov, a highly capable officer known for his leadership in the defence of Odessa and Sevastopol. Petrov was not popular with Stalin, however, and Zakharov was appointed in his place. Zakharov was described by one STAVKA officer as 'headstrong and impetuous'. However, the 2nd Byelorussian Front was the smallest of the four fronts involved in Operation Bagration, and had the least challenging assignment.

Zakharov's performance in the campaign was unexceptional, and in November he was demoted to the command of 4th Guards Army.

GENERAL OF THE ARMY KONSTANTIN K. ROKOSSOVSKIY

The most capable of the four front commanders was Konstantin K. Rokossovskiy. He was born in Russia in a Polish family, served as a cavalry officer in the Russian army during World War I and was decorated with the St. George's Cross. He had sided with the Bolsheviks in the civil war, commanding cavalry in the Far East. Rokossovskiy had commanded the 5th Cavalry Brigade during fighting against the Chinese in 1929 and led the 7th Cavalry Division in 1930. One of his regimental commanders was the up-and-coming Georgi Zhukov. During the purges in 1937 Rokossovskiy had been arrested, and he had not emerged from the GULAG until March 1940, when it became obvious even to Stalin that the army purge had been a major factor in the Soviet Union's disgraceful performance in the 1940 Finnish war. Rokossovskiy was given command of the new 9th Mechanised Corps in Ukraine. Like most Soviet tank formations of the period, it was routed by the German 1941 invasion. He was then assigned to take command of the 4th Army, defending Smolensk during a key series of battles that helped prevent the German capture of Moscow in 1941. His skilful leadership had led to his command of the 16th Army, also in the Moscow campaign. In July 1942 Rokossovskiy had been given his first front command, leading the Bryansk Front. This assignment was short-lived, and in September he was transferred to command the critical Stalingrad Front. His superb leadership there brought him into the ranks of a small group of senior Soviet generals including Zhukhov, Konev and Vasilevskiy, entrusted by Stalin with all major campaigns. During the Kursk battle, Rokossovskiy commanded the Central Front, later reorganised

Konstantin Rokossovskiy had been one of the Red Army's leading cavalry commanders until 1937 when thrown into the Gulag during the purges. He emerged from prison in 1940 to take control of one of the new tank corps and, soon after, of armies and fronts. (Sovfoto)

Due to concerns over German fortification of the forward defensive lines in Byelorussia, the Red Army brought forward a large number of heavy howitzer regiments. This is a battery of 203mm B-4 Model 1931 howitzers, one of the heaviest in the Soviet arsenal. It used an unusual tracked carriage since it was found that ordinary wheeled carriages too often bogged down due to their enormous weight – 16 tons. This howitzer fired a 100kg (220lb) projectile that had to be loaded using a special crane. (Sovfoto)

as the 1st Byelorussian Front, and in the autumn of 1943 he was responsible for turning the German defensive line at Kiev. For Operation Bagration, the 1st Byelorussian Front became a super-front, significantly larger than any of the other fronts assigned to Operation Bagration. The reason for this was its unique geographic position, astride the Pripyat marches which bisected the Eastern Front.

Besides the four front commanders, two other Red Army commanders played a special role in Operation Bagration. Stalin appointed his two senior commanders, Georgi Zhukov and Aleksandr Vasilevskiy, to oversee the operation as special representatives of STAVKA. Vasilevskiy was assigned to co-ordinate the operations of the 1st Baltic and 3rd Byelorussian fronts in the northern sector. Undoubtedly, Stalin was concerned about the lack of experience of both Bagramyan and Chernyakovskiy. Zhukov was assigned to oversee the 1st and 2nd Byelorussian fronts. There were no doubts about Rokossovskiy's capabilities, but the 1st Byelorussian Front had been assigned a particularly complicated role, serving as a link between Operation Bagration and a follow-on campaign against Army Group North Ukraine that would start once Army Group Centre had been crushed.

THE OPPOSING ARMIES

THE WEHRMACHT

The German forces of Army Group Centre were ill-prepared to face the coming onslaught from the Red Army. Due to a serious misunderstanding of Soviet intentions, the OKH did not expect Army Group Centre to face the main Soviet thrust. The heavy drain of Panzer units to France and northern Ukraine had left Army Group Centre with a primarily infantry force, very weakly supported in both armour and aircraft. The situation was made even worse on 30 May 1944, when Model managed to convince Hitler to shift the 56th Panzer Corps from Army Group Centre to Army Group North Ukraine.

On the eve of Operation Bagration Army Group Centre had 34 infantry divisions, two Luftwaffe field divisions, seven security divisions, two Panzer Grenadier divisions (plus elements of the badly mauled Pz.Gren.Div. Feldherrnhalle) and one Panzer division. There were several Hungarian divisions to the rear, but the Germans placed little hope in these formations. In total, the German armed forces in Byelorussia had the equivalent of 52 divisions, with about 400,000 combat troops and a further 400,000 in support units, administrative posts and other non-combat positions. While this was a very substantial force, it had several significant shortcomings.

Although German artillery was largely overwhelmed by the intensity of the Soviet bombardment, it was by no means toothless. This is a 150mm 'Hummel' self-propelled howitzer of the type used by the Panzer divisions; there was a battery of six per division. (Janusz Magnuski)

OPPOSING FORCES, 23 JUNE 1944

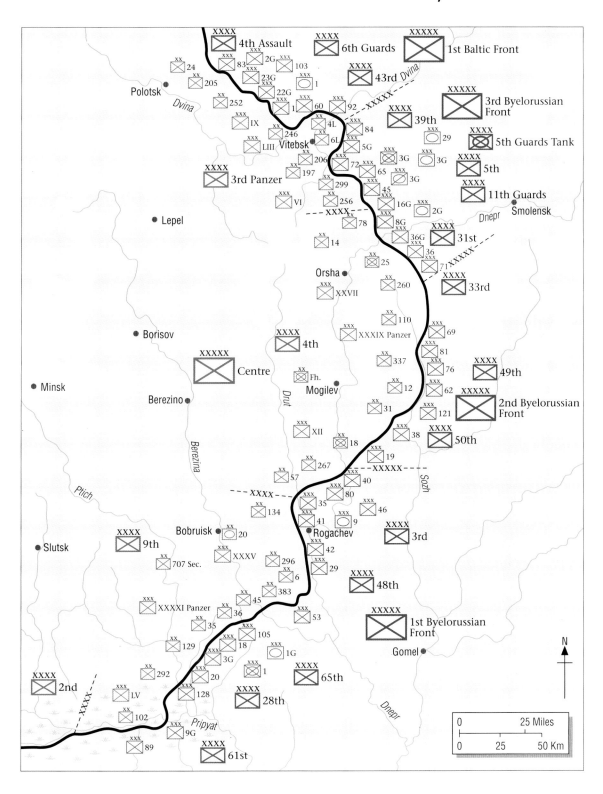

Tactical air defence for Army Group Centre was provided by a variety of weapons including the 37mm FlaK 36, seen here carried on the Krauss Maffei 8-ton SdKfz 7/1 half-track. These were generally issued to special Luftwaffe air defence units rather than Wehrmacht units.

Given the length of the front to be defended, German infantry divisions were stretched beyond prudent limits. Each division covered a front of 24–32km – about double the norm. This meant that each kilometre of front was covered by only about 80 frontline infantry, backed up on average by two or three artillery pieces and one or two assault-guns.

The low density of Germany forces along the frontline also forced Army Group Centre planners to keep a minimal strategic reserve. Virtually all of the divisions held a sector of the front, with the exception of the 14th Infantry Division, the understrength 20th Panzer Division and the shattered Pz.Gren.Div. Feldherrnhalle. As a result, once the Soviets penetrated the frontline infantry formations, there was little or no defence in depth. The Germans did partially fortify a number of major towns and cities, but these locations were weakly held by support troops.

The quality of German infantry troops had declined steadily through the war, due to the enormous casualties. Since 1943 there had been a steady influx of Volksdeutsch, ethnic Germans from eastern Europe. Replacement battalions sent to Army Group Centre in the autumn of 1943 were almost a third Volksdeutsche, who the senior commanders felt were unwilling or unable to withstand determined Soviet assaults. Even units raised in Germany contained a growing draft of Alsatians, Poles and other ethnic minorities from the fringes of the country, few of whom had enthusiasm for dying for Hitler's Germany. Although German Panzer units did not suffer these problems, increasing shortages of fuel had led to severe curtailments in training, which had a detrimental effect on their combat performance. The clear tactical advantage enjoyed by German troops early in the Russo-German war was disappearing, as German troop quality became increasingly mediocre and Soviet troop performance improved.

Army Group Centre fought from prepared defensive positions. The Byelorussian sector had been relatively static for several months before Operation Bagration, which meant that the Germans had been able to carry out extensive field-fortification work. In general, each division constructed three to five trench lines, to a depth of 5-6km. These defensive positions

ORDER OF BATTLE: WEHRMACHT
23 JUNE 1944

ARMY GROUP CENTRE
Generalfeldmarschall E. Busch

ARMY GROUP RESERVE
14 PGD, 707 SD, 20 PzD, PGD Feldherrnhalle
Fester Platz Bobruisk *Generalmajor A. Hamann*
Fester Platz Mogilev *Generalmajor G. von Erdmannsdorf*
Fester Platz Orscha *Gen. Traut*
Fester Platz Vitebsk *Gen. Gollwitzer*

3RD PANZER ARMY *Generaloberst G.H. Reinhardt*
VI Corps *Gen. der Art. G. Pfeiffer*
197 ID, 256 ID, 299 ID
IX Corps *Gen. der Art. R. Wuthmann*
252 ID, Korps Abteilung D
LIII Corps *Gen. der Inf. A. Gollwitzer*
206 ID, 246 ID, 4 LFD, 6 LFD

4TH ARMY *General der Infanterie K. Tippelskirch*
286 SD
XII Corps *Generalleutnant Muller*
18 PGD, 57 ID, 267 ID
XXVII Corps *Gen. der Inf. Volkers*
25 PGD, 78 StD, 260 ID

XXXIX Panzer Corps *Gen. der Art. R. Martinek*
12 ID, 31 ID, 110 ID, 337 ID

9TH ARMY *General der Infanterie H. Jordan*
XXXV Corps *Gen.Lt. K.J. Freiherr von Lutzow*
6 ID, 45 ID, 134 ID, 296 ID, 383 ID
XXXXI Panzer Corps *Gen. der Art. H. Weidling*
35 ID, 36 ID, 129 ID
LV Corps *Gen. der. Inf. F. Herrlein*
102 ID, 292 ID

2ND ARMY *Generaloberst W. Weiss*
201 SD, 221 SD, 391 SD, 390 FTD
VIII Corps *Gen. der Inf. G. Hoehne*
XX Corps *Gen. der Art. R. Freiherr von Roman*
XXIII Corps *Gen. der Pion. O. Tiemann*

Legend

FTD	*Field Training Division*	PGD	*Panzer Grenadier Division*
ID	*Infantry Division*	SD	*Security Division*
LFD	*Luftwaffe Field Division*	StD	*Sturm (Assault) Division*
PzD	*Panzer Division*		

included reinforced machine-gun and mortar pits, but there were generally few concrete field fortifications. The defensive belts were very heavily mined, and most were protected by extensive barbed wire barriers and some anti-tank barriers. By this stage of the war, the infantry was well provided with Panzerfaust anti-tank rockets. The principal anti-tank weapon of the division was the 75mm PaK 40 towed anti-tank gun (about 24 per division), and this was often supplemented by the division's few towed 88mm anti-aircraft guns.

German tank production continued to increase in 1943 and 1944, but it still lagged behind Soviet output. The defence industries remained one of Germany's weakest links, even after Albert Speer's 1943 reforms. German heavy industrial capacity had been significantly greater than the Soviet Union's before the war. Furthermore, Germany had gained control of much of Europe's industrial capability in the 1938-40 victories; its 1941 victories had deprived the Soviet Union of much of its heavy industrial capacity too, especially in Ukraine. Yet in spite of these substantial industrial advantages, Germany continued to be outproduced by the Soviet Union in many critical weapons categories, including tanks and artillery. This was in part due to the effects of Anglo-American bombing of German industries, but it was also due to a lack of appreciation of the military industrial needs of modern war by the leadership, and to Germany's remarkable failure to mobilise its defence industries fully until late in the war. The huge attrition of manpower in World War I had given way to a huge attrition in materiel in World War II, a challenge that Germany proved chronically

By far the most common German armoured vehicle in Army Group Centre was the StuG III 75mm assault-gun. These were used to provide fire support to the infantry divisions, and were also useful for anti-tank defence. Here a Soviet tank crew looks over a StuG III Ausf. G abandoned during the fighting. (Sovfoto)

unable to meet. This major strategic failure was to become painfully obvious in the Byelorussian campaign.

Of the 4,740 tanks and assault-guns (Sturmgeschutz) assigned to the Eastern Front on 1 June 1944, Army Group Centre had only 553 (11 per cent of the total), of which 480 were StuG III infantry assault-guns. The heaviest concentration of armour was with the 4th Army defending Orsha, which had 40 tanks (including 29 Tiger Is) and 246 StuG IIIs. In addition to tanks and assault-guns, there were a few hundred self-propelled Panzerjäger (tank destroyers), including some of the powerful Hornisse 88mm self-propelled guns. The very low proportion of tanks to assault-guns was due to the expectation that Army Group Centre would be fighting relatively static defensive battles. The number of German tanks

The most common self-propelled howitzer in German service was the 105mm Wespe howitzer, based on the obsolete PzKpfw II tank chassis. This weapon was introduced in the summer of 1944 to replace towed howitzers. The heavy foliage is no doubt due to the threat posed by the Red Air Force at this stage of the war. (National Archives)

Tactical fire support of Soviet rifle formations was heavily entrusted to mortars like this 120mm Model 1943 regimental mortar. Each Soviet rifle regiment had a mortar company with four 120mm mortars for fire support, as well as four 76mm regimental guns. (Sovfoto)

A Soviet rifle platoon in action during the 6th Guards Army attacks north of Vitebsk at the beginning of Operation Bagration. As is evident in this view, the Soviet infantry made much wider use of sub-machine-guns than most armies of the period, which still relied on rifles. In the background a rifleman with a PTRS anti-tank rifle is evident. (Sovfoto)

increased immediately after the offensive began, since the OKH began shifting tank units into Byelorussia to stem the Soviet advance. Precise figures on German artillery are lacking, though Russian sources indicate that the total strength was 9,500 guns and mortars. Under the standard organisation, each of the infantry divisions had 36 howitzers (105mm) and 12 heavy (150mm) guns. Army Group Centre was generally unhappy about the amount of artillery ammunition available.

Air cover for Army Group Centre was provided by Luftflotte 6, headquartered in Minsk. At the time of Operation Bagration this force numbered 839 combat aircraft. There were only two fighter groups in the area, which were reduced in strength from 66 on 31 May to only about 40 Me-109G/Ks by 22 June, due to combat losses. For all intents and purposes, the Luftwaffe ceded the air to the Red Air Force even before the battle had begun. Bomber strength totalled 312, nearly all Heinkel He-111s, with a small number of Ju-88. However, their combat survivability was limited due to the lack of escort fighters. Ground attack units included 106 Ju-87G Stuka tank-busters and FW-190 fighter bombers.

THE RED ARMY

The Red Army units involved in Operation Bagration were a formidable force. The four Red Army fronts totalled 118 rifle divisions, eight tank and mechanised corps, six cavalry divisions, 13 artillery divisions and 14 air defence divisions. (Figures here exclude the units of the 1st Byelorussian Front's southern wing not committed to Operation Bagration.) These units possessed about 1,700,000 troops and support personnel – more than double their German opponents.

Soviet rifle divisions were generally smaller than their German counterparts, averaging 2,500–4,000 troops. At the time of Operation Bagration a concerted effort was made to bring these units up to an average of 6,000

ABOVE *A remarkable photo of Soviet cavalry moving across the rolling hills of Galicia during the Lvov Sandomierz Operation in July 1944. The Red Army continued to use the cavalry as a mobile exploitation force through the war, and the last divisions were not disbanded from the Soviet Army until 1957. (Sovfoto)*

LEFT *An armoured column moves through the ruins of Mogilev on 26 June 1944. In the lead are a pair of T-34 Model 1943s, the most common tank in Soviet service at the time of Operation Bagration. Behind them is one of the new SU-85 tank destroyers. The vehicle to the left is a Lend-Lease Dodge three-quarter ton truck. Lend-Lease trucks provided by the Untied States gave the Red Army tactical mobility along Byelorussia's primitive road network. (Sovfoto)*

troops. No serious effort was made to bring them up to their nominal table-of-organisation-and-equipment strength of 9,600 troops: the Soviets preferred to fight with a rifle corps made up of two or three weak divisions rather than a fully equipped rifle division. The advantage of the corps organisation was that it gave the infantry increased combat support, usually adding a howitzer regiment, an assault-gun battalion or regiment, a signal battalion and a combat engineer battalion. By 1944 a Soviet rifle corps was similar to a British or American infantry division in firepower, even if the terminology was different. Likewise, a Soviet tank corps was similar in size to an American armoured division.

The six cavalry divisions were intended to provide the Red Army with mobility in the poor terrain – forests and marshes that were not suitable for armoured vehicles. Cavalry was derided in western Europe as a worthless anachronism, but on the Eastern Front it was still quite useful. (The Soviet army did not disband its last cavalry division until 1957.) The cavalry corps, consisting of two or three cavalry divisions, had substantial

Several ADD strategic bomber divisions were committed to the support of Operation Bagration, many of them equipped with the Ilyushin IL-4, as seen here. In the foreground the regiment's ordnance unit prepares a cluster bomb dispenser. This 500kg (1,110lb) RRAB-2 could carry 66 AO-10 cluster bombs.

additional firepower in the form of between two and four tank regiments (70-140 tanks), an assault-gun regiment and various artillery units. Cavalry units were often paired with mechanised or tank corps to form special cavalry-mechanised groups. These groups were intended for the exploitation phase of the campaign, after the initial German defensive lines had been overcome. They could race ahead to secure key bridges or river fords.

The Red Army enjoyed substantial numerical advantages in armoured equipment. During the initial phase of Operation Bagration there were 2,715 tanks and 1,355 assault-guns, roughly a six-fold advantage over the Germans. About 40 per cent of the Soviet armour was allotted to tank and assault-gun units attached to the rifle corps, to provide direct fire support during the penetration phase of the operation. A little over 60 per cent of the armour was contained in the tank, mechanised and cavalry units that would conduct the exploitation phase of the operation once the rifle corps had penetrated the German defensive belt.

Most of the Soviet tanks were medium tanks. The most common type was the T-34 Model 1943, armed with a 76mm gun. The new T-34-85 tank had entered service earlier in 1944, and was available in some quantity, often as much as a third of the medium tank brigades. Some Soviet units were equipped with Lend-Lease American M4A2 Sherman tanks (notably the 3rd Guards Tank Corps); generally units had either T-34 or M4 Shermans, not both. Scouting was provided by T-70 or British-Canadian

ORDER OF BATTLE: RED ARMY
23 JUNE 1944

1ST BALTIC FRONT
Gen.Army I. Kh. Bagramyan

4TH ASSAULT ARMY *Gen.Lt. P.F. Malyshev*
  83rd Rifle Corps *Gen.Maj. N.L. Soldatov*
    16 RD, 119 RD, 332 RD, 360 RD

6TH GUARDS ARMY *Gen.Lt. I.M. Chistyakov*
  2nd Guards Rifle Corps *Gen.Lt. A.S. Ksenofontov*
    9 GRD, 46 GRD, 166 RD
  22nd Guards Rifle Corps *Gen.Maj. A.I. Ruchkin*
    90 GRD, 47 RD, 51 RD
  23rd Guards Rifle Corps *Gen.Lt. A.N. Yermakov*
    51 GRD, 67 GRD, 71 GRD
  103rd Rifle Corps *Gen.Maj. I.F. Fedyunkin*
    29 RD, 270 RD
  Army artillery 8 GAD, 21 BtAD

43RD ARMY *Gen.Lt. A.P. Beloborodov*
  1st Rifle Corps *Gen.Lt. N.A. Vasilyev*
    179 RD, 306 RD
  60th Rifle Corps *Gen.Maj. A.S. Lyukhtikov*
    357 RD, 235 RD, 334 RD
  92nd Rifle Corps *Gen.Lt. N.B. Ibyancksiy*
    145 RD, 204 RD
  1st Tank Corps *Gen.Lt. V.V. Butkov*
    89 TB, 117 TB, 159 TB

3RD AIR ARMY *Gen.Lt. N.F. Papivin*
  11th Fighter Aviation Corps *Gen.Maj. G.A. Ivanov*
    5 GFAD, 190 FAD

Independent air units
    211 FAD, 332 SAD, 335 SAD, 259 FAD, 314 NBAD

3RD BYELORUSSIAN FRONT
Gen.Col. I.D. Chernyakovskiy

5TH ARTILLERY CORPS
    2 GBtAD, 20 BtAD, 4GGAD

11TH GUARDS ARMY *Gen.Lt. K.N. Galitskiy*
  8th Guards Rifle Corps *Gen.Maj. M.N. Zavodovskiy*
    5 GRD, 26 GRD, 83 GRD
  16th Guards Rifle Corps *Gen.Maj. Ya.S. Vorobyev*
    1 GRD, 11 GRD, 31 GRD
  36th Guards Rifle Corps *Gen.Maj. P.G. Shafranov*
    16 GRD, 18 GRD, 84 GRD
  2nd Tank Corps *Gen.Maj. A.S. Burdeyniy*
    25 GTB, 26 GTB, 4 TB
  Army artillery 7 GMD

5TH ARMY *Gen.Lt. N.I. Krylov*
  45th Rifle Corps *Gen.Maj. S.F. Gorokhov*
    159 RD, 184 RD, 338 RD
  65th Rifle Corps *Gen.Maj. G.N. Perekrestov*
    97 RD, 144 RD, 371 RD

72nd Rifle Corps *Gen.Maj. A.I. Kazariev*
    63 RD, 215 RD, 277 RD, 2 TB, 153 TB
  Army artillery 3 GBtAD

31ST ARMY *Gen.Lt. V.V.Glagolev*
  36th Rifle Corps *Gen.Maj. N.N. Oleshev*
    173 RD, 220 RD, 352 RD
  71st Rifle Corps *Gen.Lt. P.K.Koshevoy*
    88 RD, 192 RD, 331 RD
  113th Rifle Corps *Gen.Maj. K.I. Provalov*
    62 RD, 174RD, 213 TB

39TH ARMY *Gen.Lt. I.I. Lyudnikov*
  5th Guards Rifle Corps *Gen.Maj. I.S. Bezugliy*
    17 GRD, 19 GRD, 91 GRD, 251 GRD
  84th Rifle Corps *Gen.Maj. Yu.M. Prokofiev*
    158 RD, 164 RD, 262 RD, 28 TB

5TH TANK ARMY *Marshal P.A.Rotmistrov*
  3rd Guards Tank Corps *Gen.Maj. I.A. Bobchenko*
    3 GTB, 18 GTB, 19 GTB
  3rd Guards Cavalry Corps *Gen.Lt. N.S. Oslikovskiy*
    5 CD, 6 GCD, 32 GCD
  3rd Guards Mech. Corps *Gen.Lt. V.T. Obukov*
    7 GMB, 8 GMB, 35 GTB

1ST AIR ARMY *Gen.Lt. M.M. Gromov*
  1st Guards Bomber Corps Gen.Lt. V.A. Ushakov
    3 GBAD, 4 GBAD, 5 GBAD, 6 GBAD, 113 GBAD,
    334 GBAD, 213 NBAD
  3rd Strike Aviation Corps *Gen. Maj. M.I. Gorlachenko*
    307 SAD, 308 SAD
  1st Guards Fighter Av. Corps
  Gen. Maj. Ye. M. Belitskiy
    3 GFAD, 4 GFAD
  2nd Fighter Aviation Corps
  Gen.Maj. *A. S. Blagoveshchenskiy*
    7 GFAD, 322 FAD
  3rd Fighter Aviation Corps
  Gen. Lt. Ye. Ya. Savitskiy
    265 FAD, 278 FAD

2ND BYELORUSSIAN FRONT
Gen.Col. G. F. Zakharov

33RD ARMY *Gen.Lt. V.D. Kryuchenkin*
    70 RD, 157 RD, 344 RD

49TH ARMY *Gen.Lt. I.T. Grishin*
  62nd Rifle Corps *Gen.Maj. A.F. Naumov*
    64 RD, 330 RD, 369 RD
  69th Rifle Corps *Gen.Maj. H.N. Multan*
    42 RD, 222 RD
  76th Rifle Corps *Gen.Maj. M.I. Glukhov*
    49 RD, 199 RD, 290 RD
  81st Rifle Corps *Gen.Maj. V.V. Panyukhov*
    32 RD, 95 RD, 153 RD, 42 GTB, 43 GTB

50TH ARMY *Gen.Lt. I.V. Boldin*
  19th Rifle Corps *Gen. Maj. D. I. Samarskiy*
    324 RD, 362 RD
  38th Rifle Corps *Gen.Maj. A.D. Tereshkov*
    110 RD, 139 RD, 385 RD
  121st Rifle Corps *Gen.Maj. D.I. Smirnov*
    238 RD, 307 RD, 380 RD

4TH AIR ARMY *Gen.Col. K.A. Vershinin*
    325 NBAD, 230 SAD, 233 SAD, 229 FAD, 309 FAD

1ST BYELORUSSIAN FRONT*
Gen.Army K.K.Rokossovskiy

4TH ARTILLERY CORPS

3RD ARMY *Gen.Lt. A.V. Gorbatov*
  35th Rifle Corps *Gen.Maj. V.G. Zholudev*
    250 RD, 323 RD, 348 RD
  40th Rifle Corps *Gen.Maj. V.S. Kuznetsov*
    120 GRD, 269 RD
  41st Rifle Corps *Gen.Maj. V.K. Urbanovich*
    129 RD, 169 RD
  46th Rifle Corps *Gen.Maj. K.M. Erastov*
    82 RD, 108 RD, 413 RD
  80th Rifle Corps *Gen.Maj. I.L. Ragulya*
    5 RD, 186 RD, 283 RD
  9th Tank Corps *Gen.Maj. B.S. Bakharov*
    23 TB, 95 TB, 108 TB, 8MB
  Army artillery 5 GMD

28TH ARMY *Gen.Lt. A.A.Luchinskiy*
  3rd Guards Rifle Corps *Gen.Maj. F.I. Perkhorovich*
    50 GRD, 54 GRD, 96 GRD
  20th Rifle Corps *Gen.Maj. N.A. Shvarev*
    48 GRD, 55 GRD, 20 RD
  128th Rifle Corps *Gen.Maj. P.F. Batitskiy*
    61 RD, 130 RD, 152 RD
  Army artillery 5 BtAD, 12 BtAD

48TH ARMY *Gen.Lt. P.L. Romanenko*
  29th Rifle Corps *Gen.Maj. A.M. Andreyev*
    102 RD, 217 RD
  42nd Rifle Corps *Gen.Lt. K.S. Kolganov*
    137 RD, 170 RD, 399 RD
  53rd Rifle Corps *Gen.Maj. I.A.Gartsev*
    17 RD, 73 RD, 96 RD, 194 RD
  Army artillery 22 BtAD

61ST ARMY *Gen.Lt. P.A. Bedov*
  9th Guards Rifle Corps Gen.Maj. M.A. Popov
    12 GRD, 212 RD
  89th Rifle Corps *Gen.Maj. A.Ya.Yanovskiy*
    23 RD, 55 RD, 397 RD, 415 RD

65TH ARMY *Gen.Lt. P.I.Batov*
  18th Rifle Corps *Gen.Maj. I.I.Ivanov*
    37 GRD, 44 GRD, 69 RD
  105th Rifle Corps *Gen.Maj. D.F. Alekseyev*
    75 GRD, 15 RD, 193 RD, 354 RD, 356 RD
  1st Guards Tank Corps *Gen.Maj. M.F.Panov*
    1 GMB. 15 GTB, 16 GTB, 17 GTB

1st Mechanised Corps *Gen.Lt. S.M. Krivoshein*
    19 MB, 35 MB, 37 MB, 219 TB
  Army artillery 26 AD

FRONT UNITS
  2nd Guards Cavalry Corps *Gen.Lt. V.V. Kryukov*
    3 GCD, 4 GCD, 17 GCD
  4th Guards Cavalry Corps *Gen.Lt. I.A.Pliyev*
    9GCD, 10 GCD, 30 GCD
  7th Guards Cavalry Corps *Gen.Maj. M.P. Konstantinov*
    14 GCD, 15 GCD, 16 GCD
  Dnepr Combat Flotilla *Capt. 1st Rank V.V. Grigoryev*
    1 RB, 2 RB, 3 RB

6TH AIR ARMY *Gen.Lt. F.P. Polynin*
    242 NBAD, 3 SAD, 336 FAD

16TH AIR ARMY *Gen.Col. S.I. Rudenko*
  3rd Bomber Aviation Corps *Gen.Maj. A.Z. Karavatskiy*
    241 BAD, 301 BAD
  4th Strike Aviation Corps *Gen.Maj. G.F. Baydukov*
    196 SAD. 199 SAD
  6th Fighter Aviation Corps *Gen.Maj. I.M. Deusov*
    273 FAD, 279 FAD
  8th Fighter Aviation Corps *Gen.Maj. F.F Zherebchenko*
    215 FAD, 323 FAD
  6th Mixed Aviation Corps *Col.M.Kh. Borisenko*
    221 BAD, 282 FAD

Independent Units
    1 GFAD, 2 GSAD, 132 BAD, 234 FAD, 234 FAD,
    283 FAD, 286 FAD, 299 SAD, 300 SAD

*1st Byelorussian Front Oder of Battle excludes formations on southern flank
not committed to Operation Bagration, including 8th Army, 47th Army, 70th
Army, 1st Polish Army and 2nd Tank Army.

Legend

AD	*Artillery Division*	GMB	*Guards Mechanised Brigade*
BAD	*Bomber Aviation Division*	GMD	*Guards Mortar*
BtAD	*Breakthrough Artillery Division*		*(Multiple Rocket) Division*
CD	*Cavalry Division*	GRD	*Guards Rifle Division*
FAD	*Fighter Aviation Division*	GSAD	*Guards Strike Aviation Division*
GAD	*Gun Artillery Division*	GTB	*Guards Tank Brigade*
GBAD	*Guards Bomber Aviation Division*	MB	*Mechanised Brigade*
GBtAD	*Guards Breakthrough*	NBAD	*Night Bomber Aviation Division*
	Artillery Division	RB	*Riverine Brigade*
GCD	*Guards Cavalry Division*	RD	*Rifle Division*
GFAD	*Guards Fighter Aviation Division*	SAD	*Strike Aviation Division*
GGAD	*Guards Gun Artillery Division*	TB	*Tank Brigade*

Valentine light tanks. Heavy tanks were relatively rare, in just four regiments, with about 85 of the new IS-2 Stalin heavy tank. The Germans did not have the technical advantages over the Soviet armour they had enjoyed at Kursk in 1943, with their new Panther medium tank and Tiger I heavy tank. While the Panther tank continued to have significant armour and firepower advantages over the T-34 and M4A2 Sherman, the T-34-85 closed the firepower gap. The IS-2 Stalin tank was comparable to the Tiger I, even though lighter. The most critical German advantage – tank crew quality – had been eroded badly since 1941. High casualties and limited training had given the Wehrmacht an increasingly inexperienced force.

The majority of the Soviet assault-guns were the light SU-76M, armed with a 76mm gun in an open, lightly armoured compartment; these were used mainly for infantry support. They were inferior to the German StuG III, due to their poor armour protection, but they were available in substantially larger numbers. There were 14 regiments with about 295 ISU-122 and ISU-152 heavy assault-guns. These were most often used to reduce German fortified positions and to provide direct fire support during assaults on cities.

The Red Army enjoyed overwhelming superiority in artillery. There were 10,563 artillery pieces (76mm and greater) in the four fronts, plus 2,306 multiple rocket launchers. There were an additional 4,230 45mm and 57mm anti-tank guns, which were often used to provide direct fire support due to the absence of German armour. Finally, there were 11,514 82mm and 120mm mortars. German artillery officers were dismissive of Russian artillery tactics, labelling them crude and unimaginative, but as the Russians were fond of saying, 'quantity has a quality all its own'. The Soviet artillery was heavily concentrated in areas intended for breakthroughs. There were two massive artillery corps: the 5th Artillery Corps with the 3rd Byelorussian Front and the 4th Artillery Corps with the 1st Byelorussian Front. The four fronts also included ten artillery divisions and three multiple rocket divisions. Artillery divisions varied in composition,

The workhorse of the Red Air Force ground attack regiments was the Ilyushin IL-2m3 Shturmovik. Here a flight of aircraft of the 4th Air Army in support of the 2nd Byelorussian Front during Operation Bagration. (Sovfoto)

and included specialised types such as gun artillery, breakthrough artillery, and guards mortar (multiple rocket launcher) divisions. The basic artillery division was a formidable force, armed with 108 120mm mortars, 72 ZIS-3 76mm guns, 48 M-30 122mm howitzers, 12 A-19 122mm guns, 24 D-1 152mm gun-howitzers and 24 ML-20 152mm howitzers.

The second area of overwhelming Soviet advantage was air-power: 21 fighter divisions (2,318 fighters); 14 strike divisions (1,744 IL-2 Shturmoviks); eight bomber divisions (655 medium bombers); 16 strategic bomber divisions (1,007 medium bombers); six night bomber divisions (431 light bombers); and 179 reconnaissance aircraft. In total, the Red Air Force possessed 5,327 combat aircraft under direct front control and 1,007 bombers under strategic command, outnumbering the Luftwaffe by more than seven to one. The Soviet advantage was all the more effective due to the almost complete lack of German fighters to protect Army Group Centre, which meant that Soviet aircraft could roam at will; conversely German air-support missions were risky due to the omnipresent threat of Soviet fighters.

Two critical, but often overlooked, Soviet advantages were engineer support and logistics. The forward combat units were reinforced with special engineer battalions. Due to the extensive fortifications and minefields erected by the Germans, specialised engineer units were deployed, including mine-sweeping tank regiments, flame-thrower tank regiments and assault engineer battalions. The Red Army commanders appreciated the problems posed by Byelorussia's numerous streams, rivers and swamps, so deployed a particularly large number of special engineer bridging units. In

Prior to the start of Operation Bagration a key role of the partisan movement was intelligence gathering. This was undertaken by local partisan units as well as special deep reconnaissance units of Red Army intelligence, the forerunners of the modern Spetsnaz. (Sovfoto)

addition, normal combat units were put through special river-crossing and swamp-crossing training. Several tank units developed novel techniques for traversing swamps, including the use of fascines and ramps carried on the tanks. The scope of Operation Bagration demanded an enormous effort of logistics to keep the Red Army supplied with fuel, ammunition and food. Given the poor road and rail network in Byelorussia, the most important ingredient in this success was the availability of large numbers of Lend-Lease trucks, notably US-supplied two-and-a-half ton Studebaker trucks.

The Red Army had another significant advantage; the presence of a large partisan movement behind German lines. Byelorussia was the site of the largest and most vigorous partisan movement in the Soviet Union, actively supported since 1942 by extensive air-drops of equipment and personnel. At the beginning of 1943 partisan strength in Byelorussia had been about 150,000; by June 1944 it had risen to 270,000, organised into 157 brigades and 83 smaller detachments. This tied down a substantial number of German troops. Six security and police divisions – about 15 per cent of German combat strength in Byelorussia – had to be devoted to combating the partisans in a brutal anti-guerrilla war. Russian sources claim that the Byelorussian partisan movement destroyed 11,128 railway cars, 34 armoured trains, 18,700 vehicles, 1,355 armoured vehicles and 500,000 enemy personnel during the war. These figures seem inflated, but give some inkling of the intensity of partisan fighting in the region. Prior to Operation Bagration the partisans had played an important role in collecting intelligence on German force dispositions, as well as in periodic raiding of German supply columns and bases. In many areas of Byelorussia, the Germans controlled the cities, towns, and roads, but the partisans were in effective control of the rural and forested areas. Prior to the offensive the Red Army dispatched a large number of specialist personnel into the partisan centres to conduct deep reconnaissance and to prepare the partisans for a major campaign against the Byelorussian rail network. These were the forerunners of the modern Spetsnaz troops.

This Soviet PT-34 mineroller tank of the 116th Separate Engineering Tank Regiment was one of a number of specialized armoured vehicles committed to the fighting in Byelorussia. It took part in the savage fighting along the Orsha highway as the Red Army attempted to breakthrough the heavily fortified defenses of the 78th Sturm Division. (Peter Sarson)

OPPOSING PLANS

As early as April and May 1944 Hitler and the OKH had concluded, incorrectly, that the main Soviet thrust that summer would emanate from eastern Galicia (north-western Ukraine), opposite Army Group North Ukraine. The main debate was whether the Soviet objective would be Romania and the Balkans or a bold thrust to the Baltic. Actions in the Byelorussia Balcony were expected to be limited to a holding operation. One of the key intelligence indicators was the location of the Soviet tank armies, of which there were six in 1944. It was assumed that the tank armies would be the spearhead of the Soviet offensive, and their location would therefore determine the direction. German intelligence believed that all six were in Ukraine. The Soviet strategic bomber force had six of its eight air armies in Ukraine, further reinforcing this viewpoint. The Germans were unable to identify to where the three armies participating in the May 1944 Crimea campaign had been shifted.

German military intelligence in the summer of 1944 had been deprived of one of its most important assets for strategic assessment, its long-range

A rifle battalion of the 43rd Army during fighting near Vitebsk in June 1944. This is the machine-gun platoon of an infantry company, armed with a Maxim 7.62mm water-cooled machine-gun, in the background, and a Degtaryev DP 'record-player' squad automatic weapon, in the foreground. (Sovfoto)

aircraft reconnaissance capability. Luftflotte 6, opposite the Byelorussian Balcony, had 43 strategic reconnaissance aircraft in early June, of which only 26 were serviceable. These were mainly Ju-88s, Ju-188s and Do-217s. Luftflotte 4, opposite Ukraine, had 43 aircraft, of which 31 were serviceable. During the spring months the heavy cloud cover prevented adequate surveys of Soviet rear areas. By the second week of June Soviet air activity was severely impeding operations, and by late that month, immediately prior to the offensive, Soviet fighter patrols prevented any significant reconnaissance altogether. German intelligence, the Fremde Heer Ost (Foreign Armies East), headed by Reinhard Gehlen, was forced to rely increasingly on signals intercepts, which could be manipulated. Furthermore, the Soviets had adopted a policy of almost complete radio silence, relying mainly on land lines.

The Soviet appreciation of the strategic situation was considerably different. The German resistance in Ukraine from the autumn of 1943 to the spring of 1944 had been fierce, and the heaviest concentration of German armour remained in Army Group North Ukraine. Soviet units in the area were badly depleted and in need of serious re-equipping. The Byelorussian countryside was not as favourable for large mechanised operations as Ukraine, since its extensive forests, rivers and marshes made it difficult to move armoured formations. On the other hand, Byelorussia had a very active partisan movement, which would have a corrosive effect on German defence. Furthermore, once Byelorussia was liberated, it would place

Soviet infantry fighting on the heights overlooking Vitebsk in late June 1944. By refusing to allow the 53rd Corps to break out from encircled Vitebsk, Hitler condemned the four divisions there to certain destruction.

Germany's Army Group North and Army Group North Ukraine in a very awkward situation, with Soviet units operating to the west of their positions. The fact that it was unexpected by the Germans made the Byelorussian option particularly attractive to Stalin and the STAVKA. It is still unclear if the Soviets knew about the German strategic assessments, either through spies or intercepts of the compromised ENIGMA code. The decision to strike in Byelorussia was made in mid-April and was codenamed Operation Bagration, named after the Russian prince who had died in battle against Napoleon at Borodino.

The Soviet strategic plan was a cascading series of offensives. The first would begin in early June against Finland, to knock it out of the war. This would distract German attention, as would the Anglo-American invasion of France which was expected in early June 1944. The cross-Channel invasion would help to drain away Germany's strategic reserves, especially its Panzer units. This would set the stage for Operation Bagration in Byelorussia. Once Bagration was reaching its successful climax, a third offensive would be launched in northern Ukraine. It was presumed that a successful operation in the Byelorussian Balcony would weaken Army Group North Ukraine by forcing the diversion of units to bolster the collapsing Army Group Centre.

The key was to ensure that the Germans did not reinforce Byelorussia. The weak force configuration in Byelorussia in the spring of 1944 could be overcome, but this would become much more problematic if the Germans expected a main offensive in this region and began reinforcing. As a result, the STAVKA began a major maskirovka (deception) campaign, aimed at convincing the Germans that the main blow would come against Army Group North Ukraine (as the Germans already believed). The deception campaign was also necessary due to the enormous scale of Soviet troop movements. The 5th Guards Tank Army and 28th Army would have to be secretly extracted from southern Ukraine, the 2nd Guards Army and 51st Army moved from the Crimea, and the 6th Guards Army shifted further

A German StuG III Ausf. G 75mm assault-gun moves up to the front. The soldier in the foreground is armed with the 88mm Panzerschreck anti-tank rocket launcher, the most potent man-portable anti-tank weapon on the Eastern Front. (Janusz Magnuski)

south, to Byelorussia from the Baltic. This deception campaign would take a variety of forms. In Byelorussia the movement of troops into their staging areas would be conducted at night, and units would be camouflaged on their arrival. Tactical radio traffic by army units was minimised, and German reconnaissance flights over the area were denied. False train dispatch instructions were broadcast to suggest heavy troop movements south. The Soviets recognised that it would be impossible to prevent the Germans from assessing the correct disposition of Soviet divisions actually deployed along the frontline. Rather, the Soviet effort was aimed at disguising the heavy reinforcements being shipped into Byelorussia and the presence of heavy tank concentrations behind the frontlines.

The 3rd Ukrainian Front was ordered to conduct special deception actions in early June, to convince the Germans that the main Soviet effort was being prepared in Ukraine and not in Byelorussia. A false force concentration was created opposite Kishniev, apparently containing nine rifle divisions, two artillery divisions and one tank corps. Air activity was stepped up to make it appear that the Soviets did not want the Germans to discover the concentration of troops, but in fact German reconnaissance aircraft were periodically allowed to penetrate the air defence belt and photograph the false formations. Furthermore, steps were taken to convince the Germans that key formations such as the 5th Guards Tank Army and 2nd Tank Army were still present in Ukraine.

A Soviet rifle squad enters Vitebsk on 27 June after the withdrawal of the German garrison. Hitler insisted that Gen. Hitter's 206th Infantry Division remain behind to defend the city, but the corps commander evacuated them with the rest of the corps when the Germans attempted to break out, on 26 June. (Sovfoto)

The forerunner's of today's Russian Spetsnaz special operations troops, these two razvedchiki scouts conducted deep reconnaissance missions ahead of the main Red Army divisions during Operation Bagration. Often working in concert with Soviet partisan units, the scouts were a further sign of the maturing of soviet infantry tactics in the concluding year of the war. (Ron Volstad)

By late May 1944 Army Group Centre intelligence correctly assessed that the Soviets were preparing to strike in mid-to-late June, and the 9th Army intelligence office argued strenuously that it expected a major offensive, not simply a local attack. There were two strong indicators of Soviet build-up, an increase of over 1,850 combat aircraft in Byelorussia since early May and a steady increase in the number of artillery batteries identified. For example, 3rd Panzer Army noted the increase of artillery batteries in its sector from 243 in mid-April to 340 in mid-June. These types of concentrations were the most difficult to conceal, and were obtained by a handful of successful aerial reconnaissance missions which penetrated the Soviet fighter defences. On the eve of the Soviet offensive, Army Group Centre's intelligence had identified 140 of 168 division equivalents. However, they had identified only three tank corps when there were in fact eight tank and mechanised corps, and they missed two cavalry corps entirely. Their assessment of Soviet armour strength was only 400–1,800 tanks, when in fact it was more than double the highest German estimate. The presence of the 5th Guards Tank Army was completely missed, as were several other major formations, including the entire 6th Guards Army near Vitebsk.

Although some Army Group Centre intelligence officers argued that the Soviets were preparing a major offensive, the consensus was in support of the view of the German OKH and Fremde Heer Ost. Generalfeldmarschall Busch did not accept the more alarmist assessments, and refused to convey them to the OKH. By mid-June 1944 Fremde Heer Ost had concluded that the Soviet summer offensive could start with simultaneous attacks against Army Group Centre and Army Group South Ukraine, but it continued to insist that the main offensive thrust would come against Army Group North Ukraine. The Army Group Centre intelligence assessment of 19 June 1944 agreed, concluding that 'the expected attack along the Army Group's front ... will be of more than local importance. Their aim is to tear open the front and cause the Army Group salient to collapse at several places. However, this does not allow the conclusion to be drawn of deep objectives such as Minsk.' The lack of concern was manifest in Busch's decision to fly from Minsk to the Fuhrer's headquarters at Obersalzburg on 22 June, even though there were ample signs that the Soviet attack was imminent.

The failure to understand Soviet strategic plans in June 1944 was the second major strategic intelligence failure by the Germans that summer; the first being the presumption that the cross-Channel invasion would land on the Pas de Calais rather than Normandy. The reasons for the failure were complex. There was a growing tendency to support Hitler's cravings for a major victory by slanting intelligence assessments. German fixation on an attack on Army Group North Ukraine was partly based on the wishful thinking that such an offensive held the potential for a major reversal of Soviet fortunes on the Eastern Front. The Germans did not credit the Soviets with the skill to conduct a successful deception campaign, even though there was ample evidence of past Soviet deception successes and a growing recognition of German intelligence inadequacies. There was a lingering disdain of the Soviets as inferiors whose successes to date had been based on luck and numbers and not on skill. By late June Hitler and the

OKH were preoccupied with the war in France, and had already begun to shift several Panzer divisions from Poland to France. Busch was complacent and unwilling to buck the consensus view even though several intelligence indicators strongly suggested that a major offensive was being prepared against his forces.

The Soviet plan for Operation Bagration placed the burden on the 3rd and 1st Byelorussian fronts. The role of Bagramyan's 1st Baltic Front was to prevent Army Group North from striking the northern flank of the Soviet offensive. The 2nd Byelorussian Front was the smallest and weakest, and would basically conduct follow-up operations to clear out any German pockets of resistance. The 3rd Byelorussian and 1st Byelorussian fronts were given the bulk of the firepower and mobile units. They would converge towards Minsk with an aim not simply to push the Germans out of Byelorussia, but to trap and destroy as large a portion of Army Group Centre as possible. The Soviets were concerned that the Germans might wage a fighting retreat, thereby avoiding encirclement, but Hitler's insistence on the Fester Platz defence of major cities, his usual reluctance to permit any tactical retreats, and the lack of reserve forces to facilitate pullbacks all combined to make Army Group Centre ripe for encirclement and destruction.

The original Soviet plan for Operation Bagration had called for it to start on 19 June 1944. However, by mid-June the congestion on the railways leading into the Byelorussian staging areas west of Smolensk was causing serious delays in deploying key units. Stalin threatened the leaders of the railway system, but the main attack had to be postponed four days, until 23 June 1944.

OPERATION BAGRATION

The Soviet summer offensive began on 10 June 1944 with a local offensive north of Leningrad by the Leningrad and Karelian fronts, and was intended to knock Finland out of the war. By 21 June Finland took steps to extricate itself from the war, and a truce was arranged later that month.

The first signs of the impending Byelorussian offensive came in German rear areas. On 8 June partisan formations in Byelorussia were instructed to reopen operations 'Rail War' and 'Concert' on 19 June. These codenames referred to partisan operations conducted in September–October 1943 aimed at disrupting German railways and communications behind the frontline. The campaign was supposed to be timed to coincide with the start of the Red Army offensive, but as mentioned, the latter had been delayed by four days due to logistics problems. There was no effort to push back the partisan campaign, due to the difficulties in co-ordinating so many scattered groups.

The immediate impact of the partisan effort was less than expected. The Germans had begun a major anti-partisan operation, called Operation Kormoran, in central Byelorussia in mid-May, and the Germany security

Red Army troops look over German war booty after the capture of Vitebsk. This is a 37mm Flak 36 anti-aircraft gun on a Sonderanhanger 52 carriage. (Sovfoto)

ABOVE *This FW-190A-8 was flown by Oberfeldwebel F. Luddecke of JG 51 that was brought into Byelorussia in July 1944 in a vain attempt to reinforce the heavily outnumbered Luftwaffe fighter force. The FW-190A had a similar performance to the Soviet Lavochkin LA-5FN fighter, but technical performance meant little when faced with such overwhelming odds. Luddecke, with over 50 aerial victories to his credit was shot down and killed by Soviet anti-aircraft fire on 10 August 1944 near the Lithuanian/East Prussian frontier in the final phase of Operation Bagration. (John Weal)*

RIGHT *A Soviet rifle squad advances during the fighting for Lepel by the 43rd Army. Lepel was a small town to the east of Vitebsk, and was captured by the 1st Rifle Corps on 28 June 1944. (Sovfoto)*

divisions had managed to pin down a significant proportion of the Byelorussian partisan force. However, the partisans units did succeed in many disruptions along the railway lines leading to the front. The Germans intercepted the Soviet radio instructions to begin the rail campaign, and as a result managed to defuse 3,500 of 14,000 demolition charges planted along the railway line on the night of 19/20 June. The Soviets had planned to plant about 40,000 charges, but even though only a quarter were actually laid and detonated, it closed down rail traffic for at least a day. Besides disrupting rear areas, the partisans were assigned to co-ordinate activities with the Red Army along the frontline, to assist in intelligence gathering as well as locating and seizing key bridges and other vital points.

On 22 June the Red Army began 'reconnaissance in force' in Byelorussia, with company and battalion-sized infantry raids into the German defensive positions all along the front. These were conducted to see if the Germans were holding the forward defence trench lines, to probe for weaknesses and to ensure that the front trenches were fully manned the following day for the Red Army's planned massive artillery strikes.

Besides these probes, several divisions conducted major attacks against 3rd Panzer Army in an attempt to seize openings in the German line. The heaviest attacks on 22 June were on either side of the Vitebsk bulge. The 1st Baltic Front launched a major assault north of Vitebsk when the 6th Guards Army attempted to start a major penetration near Sirotino and the neighbouring 3rd Byelorussian Front struck south of Vitebsk, near Vysochany. The aim of both attacks was to gain jump-off points for a deep encirclement of Vitebsk. The attack by the 6th Guards Army continued until dawn of the following morning, with the Germans finally being forced out of several towns. On the night of 22/23 June the first attempts to soften up the German defences began. The Red Air Force's strategic bomber force, the ADD (Aviatsiya Dalnego Deistviya), conducted about 1,000 sorties, using IL-4 and Tu-2 bombers, against major German troop concentrations and artillery positions.

The formal start of Operation Bagration was scheduled for 0500 on 23 June 1944 and began with heavy artillery preparation all along the front. The artillery concentrations were heaviest opposite the 3rd and 1st Byelorussian fronts, each front having been allotted a full artillery corps for fire support from RVGK high command reserves. On average, each artillery piece was allotted two units of fire for the mission; this translates to 160 rounds for a 122mm howitzer – about 6 tons of ammunition. The fire plans for the four fronts differed considerably in detail, but the barrages lasted over two hours on average. Most began with a 10-20 minute

A Soviet reconnaissance platoon makes its way over the Dvina river during the fighting for Polotsk on 4 July by the 1st Baltic Front. Overcoming the many water obstacles became one of the most characteristic aspects of the fighting, due to the large number of rivers, lakes and marshes in Byelorussia. (Sovfoto)

Soviet rifle troops in Polotsk on 4 July 1944. The two soldiers in the background are towing a Maxim 7.62mm water-cooled machine-gun, a World War I weapon that was still the standard heavy machine-gun in Soviet rifle companies in World War II. (Sovfoto)

period of intense shelling against the initial German trench lines, to a depth of 6km. This was intended to crush the forward trenches and destroy the German infantry before they could withdraw to deeper defence lines. Each artillery piece fired at an increasing rate, so that by the last five minutes of the initial barrage, each weapon was being fired at the technical limit of its endurance. In some sectors this was followed by a rolling barrage directed against the forward trench lines for up to an hour; in other sectors, where the German defences were especially dense, a double rolling barrage was conducted. This tactic consisted of assigning the artillery to two groups: the first conducted a rolling barrage successively against the main and intermediate defence lines; the second concentrated only on the main defence line, beginning with the second trench line. This was the first time a double rolling barrage had been used on the Eastern Front, and it was made possible by the density of Soviet artillery in Bagration. Three multiple rocket launcher divisions and many smaller units also took part in the preparation. These fired for the first hour of the preparation, usually every five to seven minutes due to the long reload times. Their targets largely overlapped the conventional artillery targets, and helped saturate the objectives. German artillery began a meek counter-battery riposte, only to be engaged by special long-range artillery formations. German accounts of the artillery preparation uniformly describe it as being of an intensity and destructiveness never before seen during the war.

The artillery preparation was supposed to be accompanied by heavy air attacks. However, much of the battlefield was covered in early morning fog, exacerbated by the smoke and dust kicked up by the artillery barrage. The only clear weather was over the 3rd Byelorussian Front sector, which permitted 160 sorties by Pe-2 bombers. Strikes by the IL-2 Shturmoviks had to wait until the barrage was lifted. This was not of great concern to the Soviets, as the operational plan envisioned greater emphasis on ground attack aircraft later on, after the first few days of the fighting, when the lead Red Army formations would have out-raced their artillery support.

The artillery preparation was followed by the first infantry attacks. By 1944 the costly and unsophisticated massed charges so characteristic of

OPERATION BAGRATION:
RED ARMY OPERATIONS, 23 JUNE–10 JULY 1944

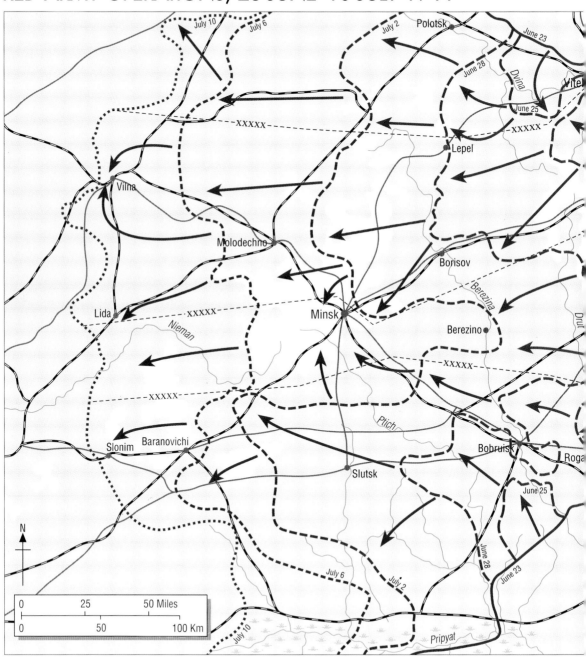

Soviet infantry in the early years of the war had been abandoned. A German 9th Army report described the new approach. 'The enemy adopted completely new tactics. He no longer attacked as in the past on a broad front with very heavy artillery support, but instead employed concentrated groups of infantry supported by highly concentrated and well controlled fire from heavy weapons. He went first for good tactical ground to establish favourable initial positions. Behind these assault groups, undisclosed until needed, lay tank forces to follow on and break through.'

By the afternoon the 3rd Panzer Army was suffering substantial inroads into its defences, and it appeared likely that the 1st Baltic Front and 3rd Byelorussian Front would succeed in a combined pincer movement to isolate the city of Vitebsk and the four divisions defending it. Generalfeldmarschall Busch informed the OKH that 3rd Panzer Army could no longer restore the situation with its own resources, and that the situation in Vitebsk was particularly serious. The OKH replied that there was little chance of receiving reinforcements from Army Group North Ukraine since the main attack was still expected there. Although the OKH considered the possibility of withdrawing the 3rd Panzer Army to a second line of defences behind the Dvina river, Hitler would permit only a limited withdrawal within the initial tactical defence lines around the city itself. The Germans were unaware of several deep penetrations by the 6th Guards Army north of Vitebsk, nor did they know that Bagramyan had already ordered the 1st Tank Corps to begin moving forward to start the exploitation phase of the offensive.

Gen.Col. I.D. Chernyakovskiy, commander of the 3rd Byelorussian Front, and his staff examine one of the downed bridges on the outskirts of Borisov during the fighting for the Moscow-Minsk highway. Chernyakovskiy was the youngest of the Red Army front commanders, and was killed in action in February 1945 during the fighting in East Prussia. (Sovfoto)

ABOVE *The German army managed to destroy most of the bridges leading into Vitebsk. It made little difference, as the Red Army encircled the city from the west, trapping the German 53rd Corps. (Joseph Desautels)*

LEFT *The Red Army managed to capture at least one bridge leading into Vitebsk. This photo, probably staged some time after the capture of Vitebsk on 26 June, shows a Soviet rifle squad celebrating their discovery. (Sovfoto)*

The Red Army was not as successful against the 4th Army, though serious inroads were made at several points. The most important Soviet objective in this sector was the main Moscow-Minsk highway from Smolensk to Orsha. This area had been bitterly contested in the previous fighting in the autumn and winter of 1943-44, and the Germans had heavily fortified and mined it. The highway defences were manned by the German 78th Sturm (Assault) Division commanded by Gen.Lt. Hans Traut, and was the most powerful German infantry formation in Byelorussia, being specially reinforced to hold this key objective. While most German infantry divisions had a 'trench strength' of only about 3,000 troops, the 78th Sturm Division was reinforced and had 5,700 troops, giving it greater density than any other unit. Furthermore, it had much heavier artillery support, including 46 light and 55 heavy artillery pieces, as well as 31 StuG III assault-guns

Troops of the 2nd Byelorussian Front move through Mogilev after its capture on 26 June 1944. The city was taken in an envelopment by the 49th and the 50th armies. The 2nd Byelorussian Front was the smallest of the four fronts in Operation Bagration, pinning down the German 4th Army while it was enveloped by the 1st and 3rd Byelorussian fronts. (Sovfoto)

and 18 Nashorn 88mm self-propelled anti-tank guns. Its southern flanks were covered by the 25th Pz.Gren.Div., likewise a very well equipped force.

As a result the 11th Guards Army attacking towards Orsha used special assault groups. These were composed of engineer and tank units specially configured to breach the most dense defensive belts. They attacked with five rifle divisions; the three southernmost divisions attacking the fortified belt were preceded by an armoured assault force. Each of the three assault forces consisted of a company of ten T-34s fitted with mine-rollers, followed 150m behind by a heavy tank regiment with 21 IS-2 or KV tanks, followed 150–200m behind by a heavily armed assault engineer battalion, followed 200m behind by a heavy assault-gun regiment with 21 ISU-152s.

General A. Gollwitzer led a break out attempt from Vitebsk on the night of 26 June 1944, but he was captured shortly afterwards. Here he talks with his captors, Gen.Lt. I.I. Lyudnikov, the commander of the 39th Army, which controlled the sector where the breakout attempt was made. (Joseph Desautels)

Behind all this armour and firepower came the initial wave of the rifle regiments, supported by a flame-thrower tank company and a light assault-gun regiment with SU-76s. As impressive as this assault appeared on paper, it became bogged down in the strong initial defensive line. Not only was there a problem with mines and tank traps, but tenacious German infantry lurked in artillery shell holes with Panzerfaust rocket grenades. Although the main effort stalled, the 11th Guards Army's two other rifle divisions successfully penetrated through a wooded area to the north without the heavy armoured support. This prompted Chernyakovskiy to begin moving a mixed task force, Cavalry-Mechanised Group Oslikovskiy, forward to exploit the gap. Busch ordered Pz.Gren.Div. Feldherrnhalle, one of his few reserve units, to take up positions on the Dnepr river line, the secondary layer of defence.

Air superiority was never in doubt during Operation Bagration: the Luftwaffe had only 40 fighters at the beginning of the campaign. One of the stars of the Red Air Force in 1944 was the Lavochkin La-5FN, arguably the finest Soviet fighter until the arrival of the uprated Lavochkin La-7. (Joseph Desautels)

The least successful of the assaults was in the south, the 1st Byelorussian Front's attack towards Bobruisk. Operations by the 3rd Army were complicated by the marshy conditions in the Drut flood plain, and the main assault in this sector did not occur until the following day. Most of the initial Soviet inroads into the German defences in the 9th Army sector were repulsed, but German casualties were heavy. This prompted Rokossovskiy to order additional air attacks the next morning, in addition to further artillery preparation.

By the end of the first day of full-scale fighting the offensive was progressing well. Vitebsk was on the verge of being surrounded, and the main road to Minsk appeared to be within grasp of the 11th Guards Army. The Germans OKH still did not appreciate that this was the main Soviet effort, so no real attempt was made to redirect strategic reserves into the area.

THE ENCIRCLEMENT OF VITEBSK

Operation Bagration had started in the northern sector, and it was in this area that the Red Army secured its first major victory. By the night of 23/24 June the 4th Assault Army had succeeded in rupturing the defences

A trio of soldiers from a Feldgendarmerie unit of the Hermann Göring Division warily scan the skies for signs of attacking Soviet IL-2 Shturmovik attack aircraft in Poland in August 1944. This elite Luftwaffe armoured unit was rushed to Poland in August as part of an attempt to stem Soviet advances across the Vistula river south of Warsaw. The Soviets managed to establish a firm bridgehead near Magnuszew, despite repeated attacks by this division. But both sides were too weak to inflict a lethal blow after hard summer fighting. (Ron Volstad)

of the IX Corps along the frontline, and in some places along the second defence belt, called the Tiger Line. The attack by the 6th Guards Army against the northern shoulder of the Vitebsk bulge threatened to separate the IX Corps from the LIII Corps defending Vitebsk. At 0245 the IX Corps was ordered to conducted a fighting withdrawal from the Tiger Line to a secondary line west of the Dvina river. By noon the lead elements of the Red Army were already on the east bank of Dvina in hot pursuit, and several bridges had to be blown, even though there were still German forces east of the river.

By the morning of 24 July it was evident to the 3rd Panzer Army commander, Gen. Reinhardt, that the Red Army was attempting to cut off Vitebsk by heavy attacks on the shoulder of the salient. By late morning both the 6th Guards Army in the north and the 43rd Army in the south were rapidly converging behind Vitebsk to the west. The whole German LIII Corps was about to be trapped. Gen. Gollwitzer shifted the 4th Luftwaffe Field Division south-west of the city to prepare a breakout operation, and requested authority for independent action. Given Hitler's attitudes towards retreats, Reinhardt asked the OKH for permission in the afternoon. This was refused by Hitler, and Field marshal Busch ordered the LIII Corps to use its two Luftwaffe divisions to prepare two breakouts, while the remaining two infantry divisions remained in place to defend the city. Finally, at 2025, Hitler permitted the LIII Corps to withdraw from Vitebsk back to the Tiger Line, but Gen. Hitter and his 206th Infantry Division were ordered to remain in the city and fight to the last. It was too late: the 4th Luftwaffe Field Division, which was supposed to spearhead the breakout towards the south-west, was encircled near Ostrovno.

With the rupture of the German defensive perimeter around Vitebsk complete, both Soviet fronts began efforts to link up and commence the exploitation phase. By the early afternoon of 24 June the 1st Baltic Front's 1st Tank Corps was on the move to the south-west, and its reconnaissance units had already reached the Dvina river and secured a partially damaged bridge. In the 3rd Byelorussian Front's sector, the 39th Army was already pushing its way to the Dvina river, and the 5th Army launched an attack on Bogushevsk, with heavy air-support from the 1st Air Army. With the German tactical defences overcome, that evening Gen. Chernyakovskiy ordered Cavalry-Mechanised Group Oslikovskiy to begin its exploitation mission. These operations left the German LIII Corps in Vitebsk completely cut-off. By the morning of 25 June the 4th Luftwaffe Field Division was surrounded at Ostrovno and Gen. Gollwitzer requested that supplies be dropped by air. Given the heavy Soviet air activity, this was never seriously attempted. The Soviet 39th Army overwhelmed the 4th Luftwaffe Field Division that evening and threatened to do the same to the 246th Infantry Division and the 6th Luftwaffe Field Division. Field marshal Busch attempted to persuade the OKH and Hitler to permit 206th Infantry to pull back from Vitebsk and assist the breakout attempt, but Hitler responded by ordering that a staff officer be parachuted into encircled Vitebsk to remind Gollwitzer that the city was to be held by at least one division. The two German divisions became isolated 10km south-west of Vitebsk, with parts of the 206th Infantry Division trapped inside the city, while the

German infantry moves forward under the cover of a PzKpfw IV tank. The PzKpfw IV was the most common German tank during Operation Bagration, as several of the Panzer divisions committed to Army Group Centre were having one of their two regiments re-equipped with Panthers at the time. The small number of Panther tanks was due to the higher priority that had been afforded the Western Front since November 1943. (National Archives)

Soviets were methodically reducing the defences with air strikes and repeated infantry attacks. By the evening of 26 June the positions of the Vitebsk garrison had become hopeless, as the Soviet 39th Army penetrated the German defences at several points. Gen. Gollwitzer decided to stage a night-time breakout, hoping that by dividing his forces, some of the troops could filter through the Soviet positions. At 0345 he sent a coded message to Gen. Reinhardt, requesting information on the nearest German positions and asking for air-support for the breakout. It was the last message received from LIII Corps and by the time the message had been decoded in the early morning hours, the LIII Corps had ceased to exist as a fighting force. Gollwitzer disobeyed Hitler's orders and instructed Gen. Hitter to withdraw most of the 206th Infantry Division along with the rest of the corps.

By dawn on 27 June the withdrawing units had been forced to break up into small, battalion-sized units. Those that did manage to slip through the Red Army positions found themselves in countryside dominated by the Soviet partisans, survivors of the savage Operation Kormoran in May 1944 who had little enthusiasm for taking prisoners. The ultimate fate of the 28,000 troops of LIII Corps is in dispute. Soviet accounts indicate that 20,000 were killed and 10,000 captured; Gollwitzer's memoirs state that only 5,000 were killed and 22,000 captured. In either event, few German soldiers from Fester Platz Vitebsk ever reached German lines.

The ferocity of the Soviet attack on Vitebsk had surprised the German OKH, which was still awaiting the main offensive in Ukraine. Hitler's

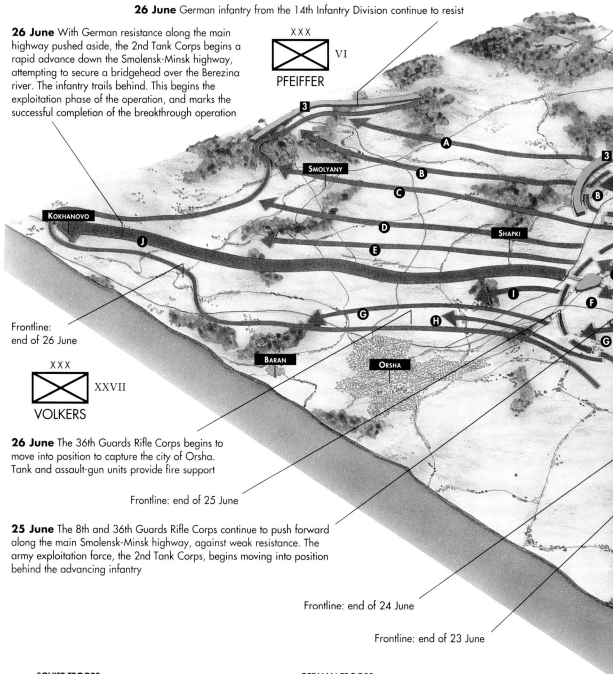

26 June German infantry from the 14th Infantry Division continue to resist

26 June With German resistance along the main highway pushed aside, the 2nd Tank Corps begins a rapid advance down the Smolensk-Minsk highway, attempting to secure a bridgehead over the Berezina river. The infantry trails behind. This begins the exploitation phase of the operation, and marks the successful completion of the breakthrough operation

XXX
VI
PFEIFFER

SMOLYANY

KOKHANOVO

SHAPKI

Frontline: end of 26 June

XXX
XXVII
VOLKERS

BARAN

ORSHA

26 June The 36th Guards Rifle Corps begins to move into position to capture the city of Orsha. Tank and assault-gun units provide fire support

Frontline: end of 25 June

25 June The 8th and 36th Guards Rifle Corps continue to push forward along the main Smolensk-Minsk highway, against weak resistance. The army exploitation force, the 2nd Tank Corps, begins moving into position behind the advancing infantry

Frontline: end of 24 June

Frontline: end of 23 June

SOVIET TROOPS		
A 11th Guards Rifle Division	**G** 84th Guards Rifle Division	
B 1st Guards Rifle Division	**H** 16th Guards Rifle Division	
C 31st Guards Rifle Division	**I** 18th Guards Rifle Division	
D 5th Guards Rifle Division	**J** 2nd Tank Corps	
E 83rd Guards Rifle Division	**K** 5th Army	
F 26th Guards Rifle Division	**L** 31st Army	

GERMAN TROOPS
1 256th Infantry Division
2 78th Sturm Division
3 14th Infantry Division

BREAKTHROUGH AT ORSHA

23–26 June 1944, viewed from the south-east showing the assault and breakthrough of 11th Guards Army

25 June A regiment of the German XXVII Corps' only reserve, the 14th Infantry Division, attempts to hold back the 16th Guards Rifle Corps, limiting their advance to about 10km

24 June By nightfall the Soviet rifle divisions are through the main German line of resistance

24 June The Germans launch a furious counterattack against the Soviet troops, south of Lake Orekhi

23–24 June Three Soviet rifle divisions fight their way through a gap between the German divisions and penetrate 10km behind the German main line of resistance.

24 June The 11th Guards Rifle Division destroys the main defensive positions of the German 256th Infantry Division

BOGUSHEVSK

XXXX
5
KRYLOV

BABINOVICHI

LAKE OREKHI

XXX
16GD
VOROBYEV

K

1

1

A

B

PEAT CUTTINGS

C D

F

2

E

G

2

H

SMOLENSK-MINSK HIGHWAY

DUBROVNO

XXXX
11GD
GALITSKIY

XXX
8GD
ZAVODOVSKIY

XXX
36GD
SHAFRANOV

L

23 June Soviet rifle divisions facing open terrain are each preceded by a special armoured assault group

0500, 23 June Forward elements of German 78th Sturm Division and 256th Infantry Division in trenches along the frontline are pummelled by heavy artillery preparation

ntline: end of 22 June

XXXX
31
GLAGOLEV

refusal to permit tactical retreats had the inevitable consequence of fixing the German defenders in place, thus enabling the Red Army rifle divisions to encircle them and destroy them at their leisure, while the mobile cavalry and tank units sped past. The large Soviet partisan formations in the area, while too weak to confront regular Wehrmacht units, were more than adequate to decimate the small disjointed units that managed to escape the encirclement.

BREAKTHROUGH AT ORSHA

The main exploitation force in the northern sector was Marshal Pavel Rotmistrov's 5th Guards Tank Army, the only tank army committed to Operation Bagration. The STAVKA hoped that Gen. Galitskiy's heavily reinforced 11th Guards Army would overcome the heavy German defences along the Moscow-Minsk highway, allowing Rotmistrov's tanks to operate along the relatively firm and open terrain on either side of the highway. As mentioned earlier, the 11th Guards Army ran into immediate trouble, even when it preceded its main infantry attack with special armoured assault units. The three southernmost rifle divisions barely managed to penetrate the first German defensive line in the first day of fighting. In the meantime the 78th Sturm Division had begun manning a second defensive belt, east of Orekhovsk. While the main fighting was taking place along the highway, a fourth Soviet unit, the 1st Guards Rifle Division, managed to push its way through a swampy wooded area between the 78th Sturm Division and the division to its north, the 256th Infantry Division. A reconnaissance patrol noticed that there was a narrow-gauge railway line running through the swamps and peat cuttings which was on firmer ground. As a result, Gen. Galitskiy ordered his main reserve, the 2nd Guards Tank Corps, to begin moving forward to assist in the breakthrough. The Germans attempted to stem the advance by a counterattack south of Lake

The Red Army had specialised river-crossing equipment for rifle division reconnaissance companies. These included the four-man LMN rubber raft and the MPK and PK rubber 'swimming suit'. The latter, seen in the foreground, included rubber trousers, to permit river crossing in cold temperatures, and paddles. (Sovfoto)

German engineers managed to destroy most of the major bridges over the Dnepr, Dvina and Berezina rivers. As a result the Red Army was obliged to erect its own pontoon bridges to move heavy equipment. This is a DMP-42 single-lane bridge being traversed by a Lend-Lease US-6 Studebaker 2 half-ton truck towing an M-30 122mm howitzer. (Sovfoto)

Orekhi on 24 June, but failed. Nevertheless, the delay in breaking through along the intended route forced the front commander, Gen. Chernyakovskiy, to order Rotmistrov's 5th Guards Tank Army to attempt its mission through the 5th Army sector further south, where progress had been better.

By 25 June the 11th Guards Army finally overcame the tactical defences of the 78th Sturm Division and began moving south-west to assault Fester Platz Orsha. The penetration of the German defences above Orsha made it clear to the XXVII Corps commander, Gen. von Tippelskirch, that it was imperative that his remaining units begin moving to the next line of defence on the Dnepr river if they were to be saved. Von Tippelskirch was reminded by Field marshal Busch that Hitler forbade such tactical withdrawals without OKH permission. However, unwilling to lose so many men due to unrealistic orders from Hitler's headquarters at Obersalzburg, von Tippelskirch deceived Busch and the OKH into thinking that he was holding firm, but permitted his units to fall back to more defensible positions. Requests to cancel the designation of Orsha as a Fester Platz were denied by Hitler. By the late afternoon of 26 June the 2nd Guards Tank Corps had passed north of the city, detaching a single tank brigade to complete the encirclement of Orsha from the west. With the fall of the city expected at any moment, a last train filled with German wounded departed westward towards Minsk, only to be blasted apart in an unexpected encounter with a unit of Soviet T-34 tanks west of the city. Orsha fell in a combined attack by infantry of the 11th Guards Army and 31st Army on the night of 26-27 June.

THE RACE TO THE BEREZINA

With the frontline defences thoroughly penetrated throughout the northern sector, and the Dnepr and Dvina river lines breached before the Germans could erect a firm defence, the next major objective for the Red

The provision of Lend-Lease trucks was an invaluable assistance to the Red Army in the 1944 fighting. The Soviet Union produced few cross-country vehicles during World War II, and depended on US trucks in the last year of the war. Here a pair of US-6 Studebakers tow ZIS-3 76mm divisional guns. In Russia after the war, the word 'Studebaker' became synonymous with 'truck'. (Sovfoto)

Army was the Berezina river. The names of many of the crossing sites will be familiar to those who recall Napoleon's retreat from Moscow along this same route.

The capture of the key rail junction at Orsha, combined with penetrations north of the city led to Chernyakovskiy's decision to commit Rotmistrov's 5th Guards Tank Army to the exploitation phase. This represented the heaviest Soviet concentration of armour during Operation Bagration, including not only the 5th Guards Tank Army, but also the 2nd Guards Tank Corps, all moving south-west towards Minsk, near the Moscow-Minsk highway. The seriousness of the situation in Byelorussia had finally compelled the OKH to begin to accept the fact that this was not some diversionary action, but a genuine Soviet offensive. Although Hitler

A Soviet scout platoon inspects a German pillbox, typical of the defences approaching Orsha. The Germans made extensive use of pre-fabricated steel pillboxes on the Eastern Front. These were actually intended for incorporation into poured-concrete fortifications, but were sometimes used as parts of earthworks, as seen here. (Sovfoto)

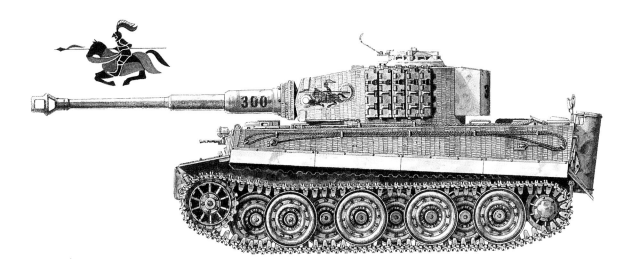

The Tiger I heavy tanks of sPzAbt. 505 attempted to halt the Soviet advances on Minsk starting with a skirmish with M4A2 Sherman tanks of the 3rd Guards Tank Corps near Krupki rail station on 28 June 1944. This battalion claimed to have destroyed 128 tanks of the 3rd Byelorussian Front, and the Soviet heavy losses led to Marshal Pavel Rotmistrov's relief from the command of the 5th Tank Army after the campaign. But by the end of the campaign, all the Tiger's of this unit were lost in combat and the unit had to be reformed with new vehicles. (Peter Sarson)

and the OKH still believed that the main blow was yet to come in northern Ukraine, they began to shift some resources taken away in late May back to Army Group Centre. The first of these reinforcements was the 5th Panzer Division, which began arriving in Minsk from Ukraine on 26 June. It was given the unenviable task of stopping the major armoured onslaught now pushing down the Moscow-Minsk highway. By German standards, the 5th Panzer Division was a formidable force, with 70 Panther tanks, 55 PzKpfw IVs, as well as the subordinate sPzAbt. 505 (Heavy Tank Battalion 505) with 29 Tiger I tanks. The division's tanks had to be moved by rail, and so were the last to arrive. A blocking force was put into position to the north-east of Borisov, consisting of the Tiger tanks, the division's reconnaissance battalion (AA 5), its infantry regiments and its engineers (Pi.89). The aim was to hold the Berezina river line and to permit the 4th Army's retreating units to withdraw in safety. The scene that greeted the 5th Panzer Division was demoralising. Large numbers of German troops, often without their weapons, streamed over the Berezina bridges. The bridge crossings were littered with abandoned equipment and vehicles as Red Air Force aircraft repeatedly attacked the retreating German columns.

The first contact with the advancing 3rd Byelorussian Front took place near Krupki, when M4A2 Sherman tanks of the 3rd Guards Tank Corps fought a sharp engagement with the Tigers from sPzAbt. 505 in the early evening of 28 June. The fighting continued through the night, with the Krupki station being captured by the Russian tankers around 0700 on 29 June after suffering heavy losses. The lead reconnaissance elements of the 3rd Guards Tank Corps skirted past Krupki but ran into the engineer troops of 5th Panzer Division preparing demolition of key bridges on the Borisov approaches.

North of the highway, reconnaissance companies of the Soviet 29th Tank Corps tried to force a river crossing of the Berezina at Studenka but were rebuffed by the reconnaissance battalion (AA 5). With this route blocked, lead tank units from the corps continued westward through the swampy areas north-west of Borisov, skirting the 5th Panzer Division's defensive perimeter.

A pair of 88mm Hornisse self-propelled anti-tank guns move forward during the fighting in 1944. These powerful tank destroyers were first committed to action in 1943 in special heavy regiments and there were 131 in service on the Eastern Front in the early summer of 1944. (Janusz Magnuski)

The five rifle divisions of the 11th Guards Army caught up with the lead tank forces on 29 June, clashing with the 5th Panzer Division's 31st Pz.Gren.Regt. near the village of Kostritsa. After a hard day's fighting the German infantry was permitted to withdraw into Borisov that evening. The Soviet 26th Rifle Division set up defensive positions on the Moscow-Minsk highway, preventing any further retreating German troops from escaping westward along the road. On 30 June the Soviet 1st and 31st Guards Rifle divisions crossed the Skha river but were prevented from crossing the Berezina east of Zembin by continued resistance from AA 5. However, several major Soviet units were already over the Berezina, north and south of Borisov. The 29th Tank Corps had managed to force the river north of the 5th Panzer Division positions, and the 3rd Guards Mechanised Corps provided its own crossing when the commander of the 35th Guards Tank Brigade ordered three of his tanks driven into the river to form an improvised bridge. South of Borisov, two rifle divisions of the 11th Guards Army forced crossings of the Berezina river against patchy opposition from five German police regiments. Further to the south, the 31st Army began crossings above Berezino, thinly held by remnants of the German 31st and 267th infantry divisions under Gen. V. Muller. By the end of 30 June the Berezina has been crossed in numerous places north and south of Borisov, and there were no German mobile reserves capable of counterattacking the bridgeheads. The Luftwaffe launched a series of attacks against the bridges, mainly using FW-190 fighter-bombers, but with little result.

The 5th Guards Rifle Division enveloped Borisov from either side, while the 3rd Guards Tank Corps tried to break into the city directly across the main Berezina bridge. A column of tanks of the 3rd Guards Tank Brigade, led by Lt. Pavel Rak, forced its way across the main bridge, but as the column crossed, 5th Panzer Division engineers blew it up. Rak's tank and one other got across, but were trapped. The two tanks and a few infantrymen

A T-34-85 lies abandoned by the roadside with a Tiger I heavy tank nestled behind it. This is one of the early-production T-34-85s with the initial D-5T gun; the gun is out of battery which may explain why it was abandoned. (Joseph Desautels)

fought a desperate battle near the destroyed bridge as Soviet units tried to break into the city from other directions. By afternoon, Borisov was engulfed in street fighting, and the surviving German forces had retreated from the city by evening. The last major obstacles in front of Minsk, Borisov and the Berezina river, had been overcome.

BOBRUISK AND THE SOUTHERN ROUTE

While the 3rd Byelorussian Front was surging towards Minsk from the north, Rokossovskiy's 1st Byelorussian Front was advancing towards Minsk from the south. The first day of the offensive had not gone well in the 1st Byelorussian Front sector due to the swampy conditions in many of the key parts of the front. On 24 June the situation changed dramatically as the main offensive was launched. The 3rd Army made a penetration 10km deep against the German 134th Infantry Division. The 9th Army commander, Gen. Jordan, received permission from Field marshal Busch to commit his major reserve, the 20th Panzer Division, in an attempt to blunt the Soviet advance. The 20th Panzer Division was only partially up to strength with a single regiment of 71 Pz.Kpfw.IV tanks; its other tank regiment was re-equipping with Panthers at the time.

As the 20th Panzer Division began to move forward, Batov's 65th Army secured an even more definitive breakthrough of German tactical defences on the southern approaches to Bobruisk. This penetration continued to deepen, and Marshal Rokossovskiy committed the 1st Guards Tank Corps to exploit the breach. Alarmed by these events, Jordan changed his instructions and ordered the 20th Panzer Division to turn around and move south instead. Its forces became tangled up on the poor roads in the area, clogged with refugees and retreating German troops. The lead infantry elements of the 20th Panzer Division forces – followed later by the tanks – met the Soviets near Slobodka, south of Bobruisk. There were a series of disjointed tank and infantry skirmishes. The Germans destroyed about 60 Soviet tanks but lost nearly half their own in the process, without halting the Soviet advance. The relentless assault by the 1st Guards Tank Corps and the Soviet rifle divisions northward to Bobruisk not only threatened the city, but threatened to cut off the German infantry divisions still on the east side of the Berezina. In the meantime the Soviet 3rd Army committed its own mobile force, the 9th Tank Corps, which began moving on Bobruisk from the east. Busch, fearful of Hitler's wrath, refused to allow the infantry divisions to withdraw westward while there was still time. By 26 June the 20th Panzer Division had been forced back to the outskirts of Bobruisk, with the 1st Guards Tank Corps threatening it from the south and the 9th Tank Corps from the East. By the morning of 27 June the 9th Tank Corps had captured the major river crossings over the Berezina from the west side, effectively trapping several German infantry divisions. The complete collapse of any German defensive position prompted Rokossovskiy to commit a cavalry-mechanised group, consisting of the 1st Guards Cavalry Corps and the 1st Mechanised Corps, to exploit the situation and race west for Baranovichi before any German reinforcements could be brought forward.

The dire circumstances in the 9th Army sector forced Field Marshal Busch to fly to Obersalzburg late on 26 June in the hope of getting Hitler to change his inflexible and costly 'hold fast' policy. The commander of the 9th Army, Gen. Jordan, accompanied him, to explain his confusing instructions to the 20th Panzer Division. Furious at the collapse of the 9th

A German infantry tank hunter team rests in an irrigation ditch while their quarry, a T-34 tank, burns in the background. These teams are armed with Panzerfaust anti-tank rocket-launchers. The proliferation of these compact weapons gave the infantry some ability to withstand tank attack, especially in close terrain. However, the short range of the weapons demanded a great deal of courage for the weapon to be effective. (Janusz Magnuski)

The fighting along the Moscow-Minsk highway near Orsha saw the first substantial commitment of Soviet armoured engineer equipment like the PT-34 mine-rolling tank. The German defensive belt on the main approach to Minsk forced the Soviet 11th Guards Tank Army to precede their infantry attacks with special armoured assault groups. This photo was taken after Operation Bagration, and shows a Polish PT-34. (Janusz Magnuski)

If any piece of equipment had become essential for the German Infantryman in Byelorussia in 1944, it was the Panzerfaust rocket-propelled anti-tank grenade here seen slung on this young soldier's shoulder. The Panzerfaust was an extremely simple rocket weapon, and was thrown away after firing. It required great courage to use since its effective range was short; the version shown here first appeared in the summer of 1944 and had a range of 60 metres. But it was capable of seriously damaging or destroying most Soviet medium tanks of the period and was greatly feared. (Ron Volstad)

Army position, Hitler relieved Jordan on 27 June. Field marshal Busch was relieved the following day, and Hitler remained adamant about 'hold fast'. This was to ensure the loss of many further German infantry units trapped by Soviet forces. Busch was replaced by Walter Model, who was ordered to report to Minsk on 29 June. Busch's previous unwillingness to stand up to Hitler over the 'hold fast' policy had infuriated the 9th Army staff, and their official diary noted, ' The news of Field marshal Model's arrival is noted with satisfaction and confidence.'

The 9th Army situation near Bobruisk was critical. The 1st Byelorussian Front had trapped about 40,000 troops in a pocket about 25km in diameter east of the city. A series of desperate and disjointed breakout attempts were made, but the proximity of the 1st Byelorussian Front's artillery concentrations turned them into a shambles. The area of the pocket nearest the Berezina river became a vast killing ground as the Red Air Force joined in the slaughter. Russian accounts claim that 10,000 German soldiers were killed and a further 6,000 captured; some escaped into Bobruisk, only to become trapped again. Bobruisk was soon encircled, and its garrison were completely cut-off. Hitler consented to shift the 12th Panzer Division from Army Group North to help lift the siege. It was understrength, with only 44 PzKpfw III and Pzkpfw IV tanks (its other regiment was re-equipping with Panthers in Germany), and did not reach Bobruisk in time to help.

Soviet infantry began attempts to capture Bobruisk on 27 June. Gen. Hoffmeister, commander of the XXXI Panzer Corps, was authorised to conduct a breakout on the condition that he leave behind one division to hold the Fester Platz, under Gen.Lt. W. Hamann. In addition, about 3,500 wounded were left behind in the town's citadel. The breakout attempt by

about 5,000 troops began at 2300 on 28 June, with a small number of surviving tanks from the 20th Panzer Division in the lead. The thin Soviet infantry cordon to the north-west was ruptured, and wave after wave of German troops spilled out of the city. But these forces were attacked at daybreak by additional Soviet infantry and tank units as they tried to reach the lead elements of the 12th Panzer Division on the Svisloch river, about 20km away. The breakout eventually saved about 15,000 troops, but they were mostly unarmed and demoralised, and of no immediate value in further defensive operations. Bobruisk finally fell on 29 June, after two days of intense fighting .

In less than a week of fighting, the 1st Byelorussian Front had captured or destroyed 366 armoured vehicles and 2,664 artillery pieces, killed 50,000 German troops and captured a further 20,000. With the 9th Army decisively smashed, the STAVKA ordered Rokossovskiy to continue as planned and move on Minsk, thereby trapping the bulk of the German 4th Army and remnants of the 9th Army in a huge pincer movement, with Chernyakovskiy's 3rd Byelorussian Front forming the northern arm.

The Germans resorted to desperate measures. The Luftwaffe had been building up a strategic bomber force of the new Heinkel He-177 Greif bombers in anticipation of raids on major Soviet industrial centres. One of these, Kampfgeschwader 1 *Hindenburg*, with 40 He-177s, was committed to the Byelorussian campaign. It took part in some ineffective raids against Soviet railway marshalling yards. In early July it was ordered by the head of the Luftwaffe, Hermann Göring, to take part in low-level attacks against Soviet tanks approaching Minsk. At low altitude these ungainly aircraft

A pair of German StuG III assault-guns lie abandoned in the wake of the Soviet offensive. The vehicle in the foreground is the normal 75mm gun version, while the vehicle in the background is armed with a 105mm howitzer. Unlike their Soviet counterpart, the SU-76, these assault-guns were fully armoured. (Sovfoto)

A German observation team uses the hulk of a destroyed Soviet M4A2 medium tank as an observation post. During Operation Bagration several Soviet tank units used Lend-Lease Sherman tanks, including the 3rd Guards Tank Corps. (Janusz Magnuski)

were horribly vulnerable to Soviet fighters and anti-aircraft fire. After a quarter of the force was shot down by Soviet fighters, the bombers were finally allowed to resume high-altitude missions. However, there was so little high octane fuel available that the bomber campaign sputtered to a halt.

THE LIBERATION OF MINSK

By late June it was obvious, even to Hitler and the OKH, that the Byelorussian operation was more than a mere localised attack. Yet the fighting in Normandy and the continued expectation that a Soviet offensive would eventually take place in Ukraine limited the reinforcement of Army

Marshal Pavel Rotmistrov (right) consults with two of his tank unit commanders during Operation Bagration. Rotmistrov was commander of the largest armoured formation in the campaign, the 5th Guards Tank Army, which had also played a key role in the battle of Kursk the previous summer. (Joseph Desautels)

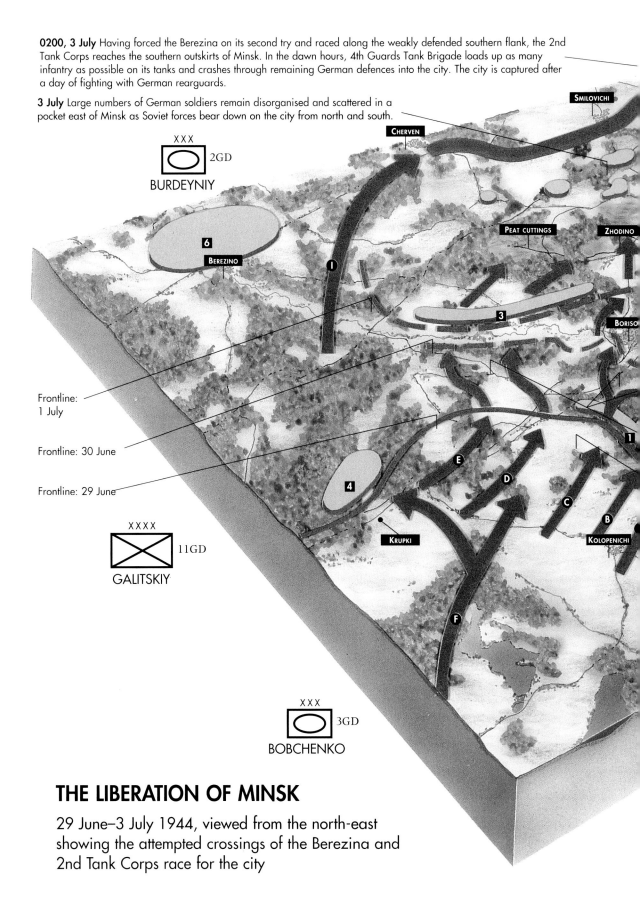

0200, 3 July Having forced the Berezina on its second try and raced along the weakly defended southern flank, the 2nd Tank Corps reaches the southern outskirts of Minsk. In the dawn hours, 4th Guards Tank Brigade loads up as many infantry as possible on its tanks and crashes through remaining German defences into the city. The city is captured after a day of fighting with German rearguards.

3 July Large numbers of German soldiers remain disorganised and scattered in a pocket east of Minsk as Soviet forces bear down on the city from north and south.

SMILOVICHI

CHERVEN

XXX
2GD
BURDEYNIY

PEAT CUTTINGS

ZHODINO

6
BEREZINO

I

3

BORISO

Frontline: 1 July

Frontline: 30 June

Frontline: 29 June

E

D

C

B

4

KOLOPENICHI

XXXX
11GD
GALITSKIY

KRUPKI

F

XXX
3GD
BOBCHENKO

THE LIBERATION OF MINSK

29 June–3 July 1944, viewed from the north-east showing the attempted crossings of the Berezina and 2nd Tank Corps race for the city

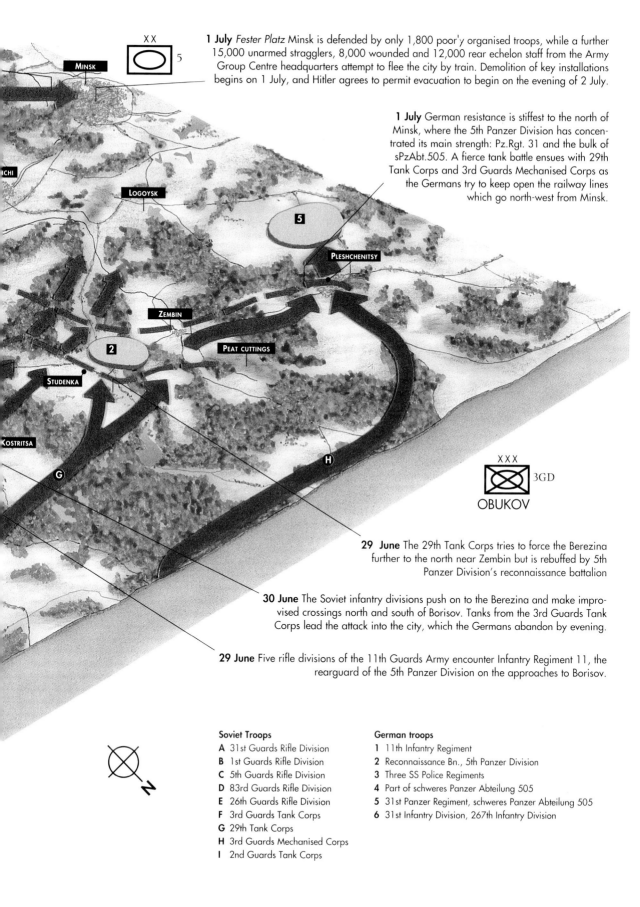

MINSK

1 July *Fester Platz* Minsk is defended by only 1,800 poorly organised troops, while a further 15,000 unarmed stragglers, 8,000 wounded and 12,000 rear echelon staff from the Army Group Centre headquarters attempt to flee the city by train. Demolition of key installations begins on 1 July, and Hitler agrees to permit evacuation to begin on the evening of 2 July.

1 July German resistance is stiffest to the north of Minsk, where the 5th Panzer Division has concentrated its main strength: Pz.Rgt. 31 and the bulk of sPzAbt.505. A fierce tank battle ensues with 29th Tank Corps and 3rd Guards Mechanised Corps as the Germans try to keep open the railway lines which go north-west from Minsk.

LOGOYSK

5

PLESHCHENITSY

ZEMBIN

2

PEAT CUTTINGS

STUDENKA

KOSTRITSA

G

H

3GD

OBUKOV

29 June The 29th Tank Corps tries to force the Berezina further to the north near Zembin but is rebuffed by 5th Panzer Division's reconnaissance battalion

30 June The Soviet infantry divisions push on to the Berezina and make improvised crossings north and south of Borisov. Tanks from the 3rd Guards Tank Corps lead the attack into the city, which the Germans abandon by evening.

29 June Five rifle divisions of the 11th Guards Army encounter Infantry Regiment 11, the rearguard of the 5th Panzer Division on the approaches to Borisov.

N

Soviet Troops
A 31st Guards Rifle Division
B 1st Guards Rifle Division
C 5th Guards Rifle Division
D 83rd Guards Rifle Division
E 26th Guards Rifle Division
F 3rd Guards Tank Corps
G 29th Tank Corps
H 3rd Guards Mechanised Corps
I 2nd Guards Tank Corps

German troops
1 11th Infantry Regiment
2 Reconnaissance Bn., 5th Panzer Division
3 Three SS Police Regiments
4 Part of schweres Panzer Abteilung 505
5 31st Panzer Regiment, schweres Panzer Abteilung 505
6 31st Infantry Division, 267th Infantry Division

A Soviet soldier examines an abandoned PzKpfw IV. Although upgraded in various ways the PzKpfw IV was in danger of being outclassed by some of the newer Soviet tanks in 1944. (Sovfoto)

Group Centre. Minsk would have to be defended with existing resources. Unfortunately, Hitler's refusal to permit an orderly withdrawal meant that most German forces pouring westward through Borisov and Minsk were disorganised stragglers, often unarmed and thoroughly demoralised. The approaches to the city were held by an assortment of small units stiffened by the 5th Panzer Division, and there were two entire fronts converging on the city. As a result, the tactical emphasis of the defence became an attempt to keep the most threatening Soviet forces at bay long enough to evacuate the wounded and administrative staff from Minsk and to protect the main railway line out of Minsk to the north-west. The Soviet armoured thrust by late June was converging on the city from three directions. The vigorous defence of the main Moscow-Minsk highway by the 5th Panzer Division's infantry prompted Chernyakovskiy to shift the bulk of his armoured strength, the 29th Tank Corps and 3rd Guards Mechanised Corps, through the forested but lightly defended area north of the city. The remainder of the 5th Tank Army, consisting mainly of the 3rd Guards Tank Corps, continued its push down along the Moscow-Minsk highway, supported by the infantry of the 11th Guards Army. The 2nd Guards Tank Corps, after an initial failure to cross the Berezina from the march, succeeded in reaching the west bank near Murovo on 1 July. It found the southern route almost entirely unprotected, and began a rapid move on Minsk from the south.

The heaviest tank fighting took place to the north-west of Minsk. The main tank strength of the 5th Panzer Division, supported by Tiger tanks

Troops of the 1st Ukrainian Front cross a river on the outskirts of Lvov during the July 1944 fighting. In the foreground, troops manhandle a 45mm Model 1942 anti-tank gun and a ZIS-3 76mm divisional gun; in the background are two T-34 Model 1943 tanks. (Sovfoto)

of sPzAbt.505, fought a costly series of battles on 1 and 2 July against elements of Rotmistrov's 5th Guards Tank Army trying to envelope the city from the north. The stubborn defence was intended to keep the Soviets away from the railway lines being used for evacuation. In a week of fighting, the 5th Panzer Division claimed to have destroyed 295 Soviet armoured vehicles of which 128 were credited to the Tiger tanks of sPzAbt.505. By 8 July the 5th Panzer Division had been reduced from 125 tanks to 18, and all of the Tigers had been lost. Both units were ordered to withdraw to the north-west.

The situation in Fester Platz Minsk was chaos. The city was defended by only 1,800 disorganised troops, while a further 15,000 unarmed strag-

A T-34-85 from the 2nd Guards Tank Corps moves through the ruins of Minsk after its capture on 3 July 1944. The 2nd Guards Tank Corps was the first unit into the city, having passed nearly unhindered through huge gaps in the German lines south-east of Minsk. Tanks of this unit can be identified by the white arrow marking barely evident on the turret side. (Sovfoto)

A Soviet motorised column moves through Minsk on 3 July 1944. The troops to the left are using a captured German Hanomag SdKfz 251 half-track personnel carrier, while to the right is a GAZ M-1 staff car. (Sovfoto)

glers, 8,000 wounded and 12,000 rear echelon staff from the Army Group Centre headquarters attempted to flee the city by train. Demolition of key installations began on 1 July, and Hitler finally agreed to permit evacuation on the evening of 2 July.

After losing some tanks to a rearguard from 5th Panzer Division, 2nd Tank Corps reached the southern outskirts of Minsk at 0200 on 3 July 1944. In the early hours its 4th Guards Tank Brigade loaded up as many infantry as possible on its tanks and crashed through remaining German defences into the city. They were followed later that day by the 1st Guards Tank Corps of the 1st Byelorussian Front from the south-east. Within days the infantry units of the 11th Guards Army and 31st Army had arrived, and the principal objective of the first stage of the offensive had been accomplished.

The envelopment of Minsk by the 3rd and 1st Byelorussian fronts left enormous numbers of German troops isolated in scattered pockets to the east of the city. Entire divisions were in the process of withdrawing across the Berezina as the city fell. Eliminating these pockets became a major objective of Soviet infantry formations for the next two weeks. During the first week of July the breakout attempts were well organised as many of the divisions retained a coherent command structure and the troops were still well armed. There were numerous skirmishes and battles as divisional groups, of several thousand men each, tried to move westward. By the second week of July the lack of food or ammunition supplies forced most of the remaining German groupings to break up into smaller detachments. These units could forage for their own food and were not as obvious to Soviet reconnaissance flights. However, they were small enough to be vulnerable to partisans, and by 9 July the largest German concentrations had been captured or destroyed. The fate of units captured by partisan detachments was usually grim. In mid-July the Red Army created special composite detachments, consisting of infantry companies and battalions supported by a few tanks and some mortars, to comb the woods for any

A Luftwaffe artillery leutnant serves as a forward observer for the artillery battery of a Luftwaffe field division. Two Luftwaffe field divisions served in the LIII Corps defending the city of Vitebsk during Operation Bagration. They were among the first garrisons surrounded and crushed by the initial assualts of the 3rd Byelorussian Front in the first days of the offensive. (Ron Volstad)

remaining groups. Isolated stragglers, nicknamed 'Ruckkampfer', continued their bitter march westward throughout the summer. Few escaped. It is estimated that of the 15,000 troops of the 4th Army caught in the encirclement east of Minsk, only 900 reached German lines.

Besides the main encirclement east of Minsk, there were other significant elements of Army Group Centre still trapped to the east. The lightning Soviet advance had bypassed several German troop concentrations on the fringes of the frontline in the 9th Army sector and 3rd Panzer Army sector. Some of those in the northern sector were able to withdraw to the relative safety of Army Group North. The total extent of German losses from Operation Bagration will never be accurately known. Germany lost the equivalent of 25–30 divisions; 17 divisions were utterly destroyed. Manpower losses at a minimum were 300,000 troops, and probably closer to 350,000. Of those, about 150,000 were captured, of which about half were killed on their way to POW camps or died from malnutrition or disease in the camps. About 55,000 prisoners were packed on trains and transported to Moscow, where they were paraded through the streets of the city under the scornful gaze of Russia's war-weary civilians. The survivors of Army Group Centre did not return to Germany until the mid-1950s, after nearly a decade in Stalin's GULAG. Soviet casualties had also been high. The heaviest losses had been suffered by the 1st Byelorussian Front, with some 65,779 men lost; the total casualties of all four fronts was 178,507 troops.

The destruction of Army Group Centre was the greatest single defeat of the Wehrmacht in World War II. In less than two weeks the Red Army destroyed more divisions and troops than at Stalingrad 16 months earlier. The sudden vacuum created by the massive losses of men and materiel forced the Wehrmacht to shift divisions from both Army Group North and Army Group North Ukraine as the Red Army prepared to launch offensive operations in these theatres.

A Soviet officer waves a red flag from a balcony overlooking the still smouldering ruins of Minsk on 3 July 1944. In the foreground are M4A2 medium tanks of the 3rd Guards Tank Corps. Although it was expected that Rotmistrov's 5th Guards Tank Army would be the first unit into the city, the 11th Guards Army's 2nd Guard Tank Corps won the race. (Sovfoto)

THE DRIVE WEST

With Operation Bagration progressing as planned, on 28 June 1944 the STAVKA passed new orders to its front and army commanders. The short-term goal of Minsk was well within their grasp, and so it was now time to think about further operational objectives. The mobile exploitation formations were instructed to set their objectives further west of the city. Following the fall of Minsk, the objectives were moved westward again, encompassing Kaunus, Grodno, Bialystok and Brest-Litovsk. This would bring the offensive over the pre-war Polish border and into Lithuania. Many Soviet commanders were surprised by the orders, since their units were exhausted and their supplies nearly depleted. But they recognised that German resistance had completely collapsed, and so they continued to push westward. The senior Soviet commanders knew that their advance would be assisted by concurrent offensives on other fronts in mid-July.

Field Marshal Model tried to reconstruct a defensive line on an axis from Vilnius in Lithuania through Lida down to Baranovichi. He hoped that old trench lines still in existence from World War I would help form the basis for the new line. It had few troops, and there was a 70km gap between Army Group Centre and Army Group North. A new army, the 2nd Army, was created by amalgamating remnants of the destroyed 9th Army and additional reinforcements, under Gen. Nikolaus von Vormann. German attempts to hold both Baranovichi and Lida were in vain; Lida fell to the 31st Army and Baranovichi to the 1st Byelorussian Front, both on 8 July. Vilnius was declared a Fester Platz by Hitler, but the 3rd Panzer

A German Panther Ausf. A tank lies abandoned in an irrigation ditch, having been knocked out in combat. Besides the glancing hit on the mantlet, there is a penetration just evident on the lower lip of the hull superstructure. The Panther was used by the 5th Panzer Division in their attempt to stop the advance on Minsk by Rotmistrov's 5th Guards Tank Army from north of the city. (Sovfoto)

Gen.Col. Pavel Batov consults with his staff during the fighting. Batov's 65th Army, part of the 1st Byelorussian Front, was responsible for the assault on Bobruisk from the south. Batov was an experienced infantry commander, having fought with the Soviet 'volunteers' during the Spanish Civil War, and having led Soviet infantry units in the 1939 invasion of Poland, the 1940 Finnish war and through the 1941-45 war on the Eastern Front. (Sovfoto)

Army was besieged by Rotmistrov's 5th Guards Tank Army on 7 July. Proposals to launch breakouts from the city were repeatedly turned down by Hitler, who again ordered that the city be held 'at all cost'. Permission to attempt a breakout was not granted until 11 July. On the night of 12/13 July 6th Panzer Division struck from outside the Soviet cordon and helped create a temporary gap through which about 3,000 German troops escaped; more than 12,000 were lost in the city. The Red Army captured the city on 13 July, followed by Pinsk on 14 July and Grodno on 16 July. Bridgeheads over the Nieman river, the intended German defensive line, were secured near Olita before the Germans could react. The fronts involved in Operation Bagration had completed their mission, and the tempo of activity slowed as the exhausted Red Army units were resupplied and re-equipped for further summer operations.

THE LVOV-SANDOMIERZ OPERATION

Hitler and the OKH had correctly predicted that the Soviets planned a major offensive against Army Group North Ukraine. Unfortunately they had seriously erred in determining when it would occur. With Army Group Centre demolished and a steady drain of resources from Army Group North Ukraine as they moved north in a vain attempt to staunch the haemorrhage, the Soviet 1st Ukrainian Front began to stir. Marshal I.S. Konev's 1st Ukrainian Front was the single most powerful front in the Red Army, even compared to Rokossovskiy's formidable 1st Byelorussian Front. In mid-July it numbered seven tank corps, three mechanised corps, six cavalry divisions and 72 rifle divisions – just over a million troops. These units included 1,614 tanks and assault-guns, 14,000 guns and mortars and 2,806 combat aircraft. Supporting this potent force further north was the left wing of Rokossovskiy's 1st Byelorussian Front, which had not been committed to the offensive north of the Pripyat marshes.

Facing these two fronts was Army Group North Ukraine, under the command of Col.Gen. Josef Harpe, with five Panzer divisions, one motorised division and 34 infantry divisions. Army Group North Ukraine had actually been fairly close in strength to the 1st Ukrainian Front through the early summer, but as units were pulled out to stem the tide in Byelorussia, the force disparity grew in favour of the Red Army. In mid-July Army Group North Ukraine possessed 900,000 troops, 900 tanks and Assault guns, 6,000 guns and 700 aircraft. The long interlude since the winter battles had allowed the Germans to establish a dense defensive belt, about 30km deep, with three main defensive lines. In addition, the towns of Vladimir Volynskiy, Brody, Zolochev, Rava Russkaya and Stanislav were fortified to permit prolonged defence. The heaviest German force concentration, the III Panzer Corps, was deployed from Brody to Lvov, which was expected to be the central axis of an attack in the area.

The heavy concentration of forces by the 1st Ukrainian Front made any strategic deception operation, such as the masking of Operation Bagration, impossible. Instead the Soviets attempted to convince the Germans that the main thrust would emanate from the southern wing, towards Stanislav, rather than against Lvov. This effort was only partially successful. The Germans did not detect that the 1st Guards Tank Army had been shifted northwards, and they missed several other new force concentrations. Besides the main thrust against Lvov, Konev planned a significant secondary drive by the 3rd Guards Army.

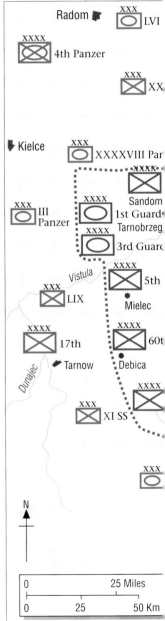

The crew of a Soviet SU-76M assault-gun wait in ambush along the edge of woods in Byelorussia in 1944. These open-topped assault-guns were mainly intended to provide direct artillery fire support to infantry units, but had a secondary role as anti-tank vehicles. (Joseph Desautels)

The Germans fully appreciated Soviet assault tactics, so around 12 July they began pulling forward-deployed infantry out of the forward defensive trenches rather than allow them to be subjected to a pulverising Soviet artillery strike when the offensive began. The Soviets caught wind of this move, and Konev decided to forego the usual artillery preparation. The attacks began on 13 July, with infantry assaults by the 3rd Guards Army

THE LVOV-SANDOMIERZ OFFENSIVE, JULY-AUGUST 1944

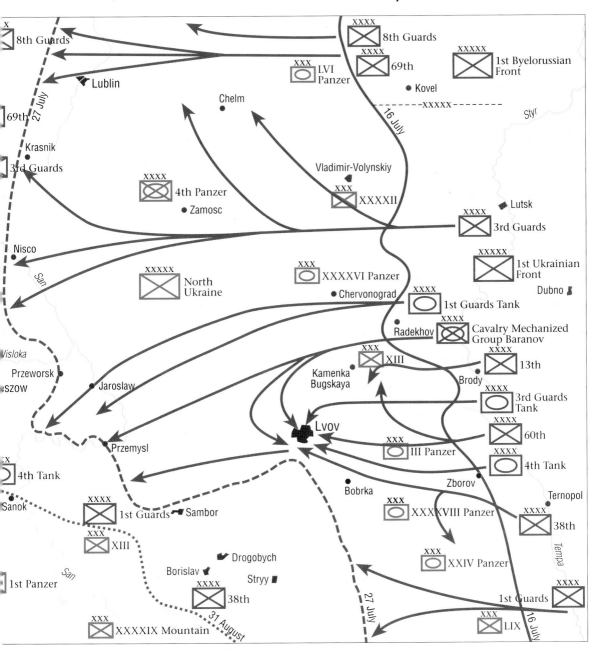

on the right and the 13th Army on the left. The fighting was considerably different from the Byelorussian campaign, with the German defenders receiving vigorous air and artillery support. After two days of intense fighting the German defences around Brody were finally overcome and the city was surrounded. Konev committed the Cavalry-Mechanised Group Baranov through a gap in the German lines created by the 13th Army, and Katukov's 1st Guards Tank Army, one of the few major Soviet units concealed by the deception plan, was launched further north.

The German defence to the east of Lvov continued to hold, and Gen. Harpe committed his main tactical reserve, the 1st and 8th Panzer divisions on 14 and 15 July in an attempt to smother the offensive. Konev had been warned by STAVKA not to commit his main tank forces, the 3rd Guards and 4th Guards Tank armies, until an adequate penetration of German defence had been made by the infantry, but the intensity of the German defensive efforts had convinced him that this was the only way to secure a deep breakthrough. On 16 July he gambled, and pushed the 3rd Guards Tank Army through a gap known as the Koltov Corridor; the 4th Tank Army followed the next day. By 17 July armoured and cavalry spearheads had reached the outskirts of Lvov, despite furious tank battles still raging east of the city as the Germans tried to seal off the Soviet armoured thrust.

On 18 July Army Group North Ukraine was hit by a second major blow as the southern wing of Rokossovskiy's 1st Byelorussian Front went over to the offensive around Kovel. The attack began with a short but intense

Streams of German prisoners are led east on the Moscow-Minsk highway after the fall of Minsk on 3 July. The Soviet capture of Minsk left nearly 100,000 German troops caught in several large pockets east of the city. They were gradually reduced or eliminated in the first two weeks of July. In the background a Soviet tractor tows an artillery limber with the barrel for a 203mm howitzer. (Sovfoto)

Axis reinforcements move forward in Galicia during the summer of 1944. In the foreground is a German Panzerjäger 38(t) with 75mm PaK 40 gun. Further along on the road are a Hungarian Turan tank and Csaba armoured car of the Hungarian 2nd Armoured Division. The Hungarian armoured units were poorly equipped due to short-sighted German armaments policies regarding its allied armies. The Hungarian Turan was armed with only a 40mm gun, hopelessly inadequate against Soviet tanks of the period. (Ivan Bajtos)

artillery barrage. In two days the German tactical defences were overcome, and 69th Army and 8th Guards Army were streaming towards the western Bug river and the key Polish city of Lublin. On 20 July German officers made an attempt on Hitler's life, which failed. The attempted assassination had no immediate impact on the fighting in Ukraine, but the enormous loss of life in Byelorussia, the attempted coup and the Anglo-American offensive in France all helped convince many senior German officers that the war was inevitably lost. The demoralising consequence of the past month's events had undermined the morale of many German units.

Konev's assault on Lvov was slower than hoped. The plan to seize the city on the march by a quick tank assault failed when Rybalko's 3rd Tank Army became bogged down by heavy rain in the peat marshes north of the city. Gen. Harpe reinforced Lvov with several infantry divisions from Stanislav. Konev did not want to tie down his main exploitation force, the 3rd and 4th Guards Tank armies, in a siege of Lvov, since the Germans would in the meantime undoubtedly set up more formidable defensive lines along the San river, further west. But the tide began to turn. The encircled city of Brody finally gave up on 22 July, netting the Red Army another 30,000 prisoners and freeing up rifle divisions for the Lvov fighting. Furthermore, Katukov's 1st Guards Tank Army was advancing more rapidly than expected towards the San river. Konev moved the 4th Guards Tank Army against Lvov from the south, and as the rifle divisions caught up, he prepared for a major assault on Lvov on 24 July. Avoiding the fate of so many Wehrmacht units in Byelorussia, the Lvov garrison broke out

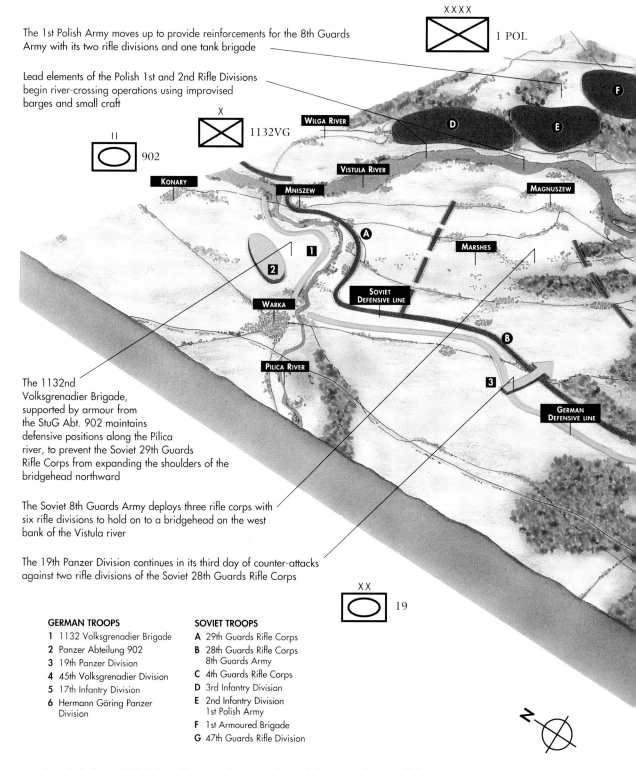

The 1st Polish Army moves up to provide reinforcements for the 8th Guards Army with its two rifle divisions and one tank brigade

Lead elements of the Polish 1st and 2nd Rifle Divisions begin river-crossing operations using improvised barges and small craft

XXXX
1 POL

X
1132VG

II
902

WILGA RIVER

VISTULA RIVER

KONARY

MNISZEW

MAGNUSZEW

A

MARSHES

1

2

SOVIET
DEFENSIVE LINE

WARKA

B

The 1132nd
Volksgrenadier Brigade,
supported by armour from
the StuG Abt. 902 maintains
defensive positions along the Pilica
river, to prevent the Soviet 29th Guards
Rifle Corps from expanding the shoulders of the
bridgehead northward

PILICA RIVER

3

GERMAN
DEFENSIVE LINE

The Soviet 8th Guards Army deploys three rifle corps with six rifle divisions to hold on to a bridgehead on the west bank of the Vistula river

The 19th Panzer Division continues in its third day of counter-attacks against two rifle divisions of the Soviet 28th Guards Rifle Corps

XX
19

D   **E**   **F**

GERMAN TROOPS
1 1132 Volksgrenadier Brigade
2 Panzer Abteilung 902
3 19th Panzer Division
4 45th Volksgrenadier Division
5 17th Infantry Division
6 Hermann Göring Panzer
   Division

SOVIET TROOPS
A 29th Guards Rifle Corps
B 28th Guards Rifle Corps
   8th Guards Army
C 4th Guards Rifle Corps
D 3rd Infantry Division
E 2nd Infantry Division
   1st Polish Army
F 1st Armoured Brigade
G 47th Guards Rifle Division

N

THE GERMAN COUNTER-ATTACK ON THE MAGNUSZEW BRIDGEHEAD

8 August 1944, viewed from the south-west showing German attacks on the bridgehead and Soviet efforts to reinforce their position

The Soviet 47th Guards Rifle Division takes up defensive positions along the left shoulder of the bridgehead area to prevent German counterattacks across the river

XXXX
8GD

The 45th Volksgrenadier Division continues its fourth day of attacks against two Soviet rifle divisions of the 4th Guards Rifle Corps firmly entrenched in woods and villages

The 17th Infantry Division holds defensive positions along the Vistula river to prevent further Soviet encroachments

PROMNIK RIVER

MACIEJOWICE

VIERZBIE

G

5

KOZIENICE

IANKI

4

GRABNOWOLA

C

MARJAMPOL

BRZOZA

RADOMKA RIVER

6

XX
17

ZYN

XX
45VG

WOLA GORYNSKA

Panzer Division Hermann Göring moves north-eastwards to help support the attacks against the Magnuszew bridgehead

RAILROAD

XX
HERMANN
GÖRING

A late production PzKpfw IV Ausf. G with added glacis armour lays abandoned after Operation Bagration. German tank units seldom distinguished the many subvariants of PzKpfw IV tanks, usually referring to these later types with the KwK40 L/48 gun as PzKpfw IV (lang) due to its longer barrel. This type was still an even match with the Soviet T-34 in 1944. (Sovfoto)

on the night of 26 July, south-west into the Carpathian Mountains. Lvov was cleared of rearguard German forces by 27 July. The same day, the fortified city of Przemysl was rapidly captured by lead elements of the 3rd Guards Tank Army, supported to the north by the 1st Guards Tank Army.

The successes in the south against Lvov, combined with the steady advances by the 3rd Guards Army and Rokossovskiy's 1st Byelorussian Front, put the Red Army within striking distance of the key natural defensive line in the northern sector, the Vistula river. By late July Rokossovskiy's forces had approached the east bank of the Vistula. They secured a significant bridgehead at Magnuszew on 27 July and reached the Praga suburb of Warsaw on 1 August 1944.

The Soviet 1st Baltic Front captured Vilnius, the current capital of Lithuania, on 13 July 1944. Here a German 88mm FlaK 36 anti-aircraft gun lays abandoned after the fighting. (Sovfoto)

The initial bridgeheads over the San and Vistula rivers were gained by infantry units using rubber inflatable rafts. This example is called an LMN (small rubber boat), and was designed to accommodate five troops. (Sovfoto)

In a final surge, Konev's forces moved on the Vistula river barrier from the march, securing several small bridgeheads and eventually a major bridgehead at Sandomierz. By the beginning of August the 1st Ukrainian Front had pushed Army Group North Ukraine out of Galicia, forcing part of it into the Carpathian Mountains and the other part to the west banks of the Vistula. Unlike Army Group Centre, it was still in fighting spirits, and was putting up determined resistance all along the Vistula. The Lvov-Sandomierz offensive had not secured the enormous destruction inflicted on Army Group Centre, but then Soviet casualties were more modest too – about 65,000.

The Soviet advance on the Vistula had untoward political consequences. The Polish resistance movement, the Home Army, conducted a partisan offensive, dubbed 'Operation Storm', in advance of the Soviet offensive in the hopes of securing Soviet political recognition for the policies of the Polish exile government in London. The Home Army actions were hardly noticed by the Red Army, and the Soviets began rounding up Polish partisans and impressing them into service with the pro-Soviet Polish People's Army. Stalin had no sympathy for the Polish government in London, since it would not acquiesce to the Soviet seizure of eastern Poland in 1939 when the Soviet Union had been allied to Germany. Stalin had created a rival Communist puppet government under Boleslaw Bierut, which was put in charge of Poland when the Red Army reached Lublin in July 1944. Out of desperation, the Home Army decided to liberate Warsaw on its own as soon as the Red Army approached the city. The objective was to demonstrate that the government in London was the genuine representative of Poland. They captured much of the city on 1 August. But the uprising had not been part of long-term Home Army plans, and as a result the insurgents were ill-prepared and poorly armed. The Home Army leaders, isolated through four long and brutal years of occupation, clung to the illusion that the Red Army would need the city to carry out its further operations.

A German Tiger I heavy tank lies abandoned after having been knocked out in fighting in Poland during the battles for the Vistula bridgeheads. Behind it is one of the new King Tiger heavy tanks first introduced into combat in Poland in July 1944. (Janusz Magnuski)

On 13 July 1944 the 1st Ukrainian Front began the Lvov-Sandomierz offensive against the German Army Group North Ukraine. Here the Soviet front commander, Marshal Ivan Konev, examines a map of the operation with his chief of staff, Gen. Matvei Zakharov. (Sovfoto)

However, Warsaw was not a major objective of the summer offensive. Stalin was brutally realistic and decided to let the Germans eliminate his political rivals. He refused to assist the insurgents until forced into some token gestures in September by British and American protests.

Hitler, enraged by the stunning summer defeats and the 20 July assassination attempt, ordered the city retaken and the Poles punished. The uprising was crushed by early October, at the cost of over 200,000 Polish lives, and the Germans razed the city to the ground in revenge. Although of little immediate military consequence, the tragic Warsaw uprising was the spark that ignited the Cold War. British and American leaders were aghast at Stalin's cruel mockery of the embattled anti-Nazi resistance movement, and at his shameless refusal to provide any real assistance as the 1st Byelorussian Front sat idle on the other side of the Vistula river.

STRATEGIC SITUATION ON THE EASTERN FRONT, 23 AUGUST 1944

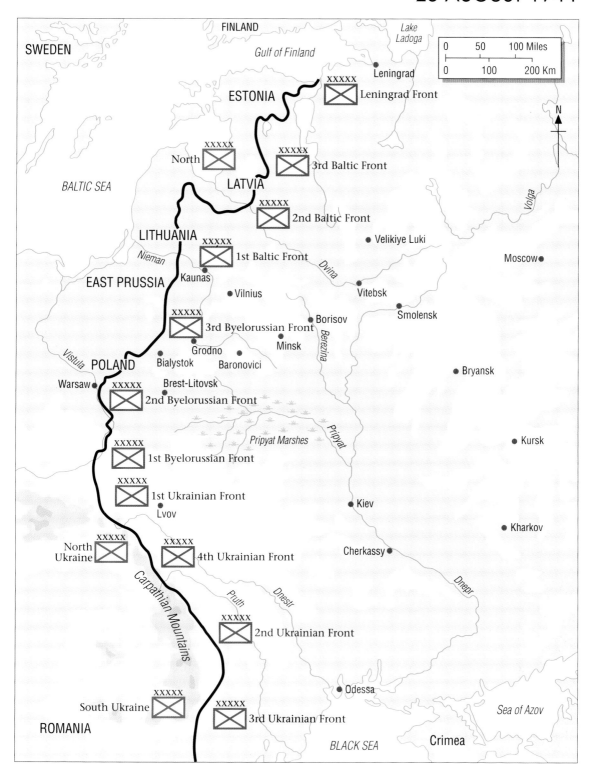

AFTERMATH

The successful conclusion of the Byelorussian and northern Ukrainian offensives in August brought fighting in these sectors to an end. The Germans began heavy reinforcement of the Vistula river line, recognising that the Polish plains represented the quickest route to Berlin. By August the Red Army units in Poland were spent, and in need of replacement, rebuilding and re-equipping. The fronts committed to Operation Bagration did not resume their offensive operations until 12 January 1945, with the beginning of the Vistula-Oder Operation, the first stage in the attack on Berlin in 1945.

The STAVKA turned its attention to other objectives in the northern and southern theatres. In the north the 1st, 2nd and 3rd Baltic fronts engaged in a series of attacks against Army Group North in the Baltic republics, beginning on 14 September, and eventually ending in East Prussia. In October the Karelian Front passed through Finland, chasing the German forces into the Arctic, and launching attacks against the Wehrmacht in northern Norway, near Petsamo and Kirkenes. In southern

Commander of the 4th Guards Tank Army, Gen.Lt. Pavel Poluboyarov oversees his unit's passage near Brody during the Lvov Sandomierz operation on 14 July 1944. To his right is Col. Nikolai Dushak, who commanded the 12th Guards Tank Brigade during this operation. Poluboyarov first saw combat during the war with Japan in 1938-39, and after the war headed the Soviet tank forces from 1954 to 1969. (Sovfoto)

A Soviet 'razvedchik' scout team moves through a Polish village during the Lvov-Sandomierz operation in July 1944. Notice that the scout to the left is armed with a captured German MP.38 Schmeisser machine-pistol, a popular weapon in scout units. Ironically, German scout units liked to use the Soviet PPSh machine-pistol. (Sovfoto)

Ukraine the 2nd and 3rd Ukrainian fronts began the Yeasty-Kishniev operation on 20 August, aimed at knocking Romania and Bulgaria out of the war. This theatre would be the major centre of Soviet attention through the autumn and early winter, and the advance reached Hungary in late October. In September the 1st Ukrainian Front, supported by the new 4th Ukrainian Front, began major operations to reduce German forces in the Carpathian Mountains.

Could the disaster in Byelorussia have been avoided? The problems were not only Hitler's. The intelligence failure underlying the surprise attack was widely shared among German army intelligence and many Wehrmacht commanders. The ability of the Red Army to mask such a heavy concentration of forces in Byelorussia had made an initial success in breaching the tactical defences of Army Group Centre almost certain. Had Hitler not insisted on the units holding firm along the frontline, it is possible that the Tiger line and other defensive lines further west could have been more effectively contested, limiting the exploitation of the breaches by the Soviet tank and cavalry forces. Nevertheless, it is worth noting that the much better equipped Army Group North Ukraine was routed in two weeks of fighting. The key difference was that Army Group North Ukraine did not suffer the enormous loss in men and materiel since they were permitted to withdraw in good order. Hitler's mistakes accelerated the defeat of Army Group Centre and ensured that more troops than necessary were captured. However, given the disparity in forces and the growing capabilities of the Red Army, the defeat in Byelorussia was likely from the start.

CHRONOLOGY

1943

5–23 July – The Germans launch Operation Citadel against the Kursk-Orel bulge. The offensive is thwarted, and Germany loses the strategic initiative on the Eastern Front.

3–23 August – The Red Army launches Operation Rumyantsev in the Belgorod-Kharkov area as the first stage in liberating Ukraine.

7 August–2 October – The Red Army stages Operation Suvorov against Army Group Centre, capturing Smolensk.

10 September–9 October – The Red Army launches its offensive on the Black Sea at Novorossisk and the Taman peninsula, eventually isolating the German garrison on the Crimean peninsula.

26 September–20 December – The Red Army stages its drive on the Dnepr river in Ukraine, clearing most of the east bank of German forces.

A T-34-85 tank crosses the western Bug river during the Lvov-Sandomierz operation. Although there were some improvised attempts to use deep wading trucks for river-crossing operations during 1944, tanks usually needed a shallow ford or engineer equipment to cross major rivers. (Sovfoto)

The crew of a Hanomag SdKfz 251 Ausf D armoured personnel carrier anxiously scan the skies during the fighting to the west of the Prut river in July 1944. By this stage of the war, the Red Air Force enjoyed air superiority by default, since there were so few German fighters operational on the Eastern Front. This half-track is configured as a command vehicle, as is evident from the added radio antennas. (Jospeh Desautels)

1944

24 December 1943–17 April 1944 – The Red Army stages a major winter offensive to secure the west bank of the Dnepr and liberate most of western Ukraine up to the Carpathian Mountains and the Polish and Romanian borders.

OPERATION BAGRATION

19 June – The Soviet partisan forces are ordered to begin their campaign against German rail and communication lines in occupied Byelorussia.

22 June – The Red Army begins 'reconnaissance in force' in an attempt to gain inroads into German defences before the main offensive begins.

23 June – Operation Bagration is launched at 0500 with an intense two-hour artillery barrage; heavy inroads are made around Vitebsk.

26 June – The Vitebsk garrison breaks out of the Soviet encirclement only to be destroyed piecemeal in the succeeding days. Orsha also falls that evening. Bobruisk is surrounded.

27 June – The Bobruisk garrison breaks out.

28 June – Field Marshal Busch is sacked and replaced by Field Marshal Model. STAVKA orders the fronts to aim further west in their exploitation efforts.

30 June – The 3rd Byelorussian fronts gains several bridgeheads over the Berezina river. Borisov is captured.

3 July – Minsk is captured. Most of Army Group Centre is trapped east of the city by advancing Soviet columns.

4–9 July – Soviet rifle divisions clear out large pockets of surrounded German troops east of Minsk.

8 July – Lida and Baranovichi are captured. Vilnius is encircled.

13 July – The 1st Ukrainian Front launches its offensive against Army Group North Ukraine

13–16 July – The cities of Vilnius, Pinsk and Grodno are captured. Bridgeheads over the Nieman river are secured near Olita.

18 July – The southern wing of the 1st Byelorussian Front launches it offensive against Army Group North Ukraine.

20 July – German generals attempt to assassinate Hitler.

22 July – The encircled city of Brody surrenders.

26–27 July – The Germans break out of Lvov and the city is captured. The fortress city of Przemysl is captured.

27 July – A major bridgehead over the Vistula river is secured at Magnuszew.

AFTERMATH

1 August – The Warsaw uprising begins.

20–29 August – The Red Army launches an offensive into Romania; the latter switches sides.

8 September–28 October – The Red Army launches an offensive into the eastern Carpathians towards Slovakia.

14 September–24 November – A major offensive begins against Army Group North in the Baltic.

Soviet infantry fight for a rail junction in the Carpathian foothills during the Lvov-Sandomierz offensive. The soldier in the foreground tending the wounded is armed with a captured MP.38 Schmeisser machine-pistol. (Sovfoto)

WARGAMING OPERATION BAGRATION

The destruction of Army Group Centre provides a wide choice of wargames scenarios. At one end of the scale, it is possible to capture the sweeping drama of one of the largest land battles of all time. Several commercial boardgames cover the entire campaign, and it lends itself to the 'megagame' format in which upwards of 100 wargamers operate in separate 'command cells', connected by telephones; while an umpire team presides over the master map. For wargamers more at home with half-a-dozen desperate men, armed with sub-machine guns and satchel charges, there are endless possibilities for tactical rather than strategic wargames: daring partisan raids on the German rail net or equally desperate attempts to escape to the west by encircled Germans.

The Eastern Front is probably only second to the American Civil War as a subject for commercial boardgames. Operation Bagration was first covered by Jim Dunnigan's 1973 SPI game, *The Destruction of Army Group Centre* and then by the 1982 GDW game *Red Army*. The latter requires rather more room: with four 17 x 22 inch maps and a playing time not far removed from the real operation, this is a typical game of its time. It should also be noted that many Eastern Front boardgames, especially the older ones are based almost entirely on German sources. At the time they were designed, academic contacts and access to Soviet sources were extremely limited. The Germans may have lost the war, but they were winning the battle of the historians. Von Manstein's *Lost Victories,* von Mellenthin's *Panzer Battles* and Guderian's *Panzer Leader* influenced and inspired a generation of game designers. Only in the last ten years or so has a more balanced picture emerged.

One operational game designed in the light of new research is *Lost Victory* (GMT games, 1994), a simulation of von Manstein's famous counter-offensive around Kharkov, February-March 1943. David R Ritchie's game system is very slick indeed, replicating the strengths and weaknesses of the German and Russian armies far more successfully than most previous games. Adapting this system to the destruction of Army Group Centre would be quite straightforward, although the scales would have to be adjusted.

Operation Bagration is included as a scenario in most strategic games covering the entire Eastern Front and space precludes an examination of all

The Panther Ausf. G tanks of Pz.Rgt. 31, 5.Pz.Div. conducted a skilled, but ultimately futile attempt to stem the advance of the Soviet 29th Tank Corps during the assault on Minsk. Although they inflicted heavy casulties on the Red Army in several intense tank skirmishes north-east of the city, their efforts proved in vain as the T-34 tanks of the Soviet 2nd Guard Tank Corps exploited a gap in the crumbling German defenses and made a mad dash for the city. The inset drawing shows the regiment's devil insignia as painted on turret. (David E. Smith)

of them. However, only those grand strategy games which employ a 'double blind' or similar concealment system adequately reflect the situation at the beginning of the campaign. The German army was deployed to meet another attack in the Ukraine. Given the stunning success of the Soviet winter offensive, it was not unreasonable to expect a follow-up in the same area. Yet as we have seen, Russian deception measures proved just as successful as those preceding the Allied landings in Normandy, Hitler's baleful influence compounding an already erroneous intelligence appreciation in both cases. So in June 1944 the German army was deployed to meet an amphibious invasion in the Pas de Calais and a Russian offensive in the Ukraine; two strategic blunders which Germany would never recover from. Those boardgames in which all counters are on the map, where everyone can see them, miss this vital aspect of the war.

The destruction of Army Group Centre drove the German armies back to the scene of their first victory in World War II: Poland. And the arrival of Russian forces on the banks of the Vistula triggered the most tragic battle of the entire conflict, the Warsaw Uprising. This has been covered by several boardgames, but the best is generally accepted to be John Prados' *Warsaw Rising*, which was published as an issue game by *Strategy & Tactics* magazine (#107) in 1986. For heroism and inhuman savagery, the battle for Warsaw has few equals. While the military stages of the struggle can be recreated with maps and cardboard counters, the famous Polish film *Kanal* is compulsory viewing.

A group of Soviet riflemen assault a German position inside a Polish farmhouse during the Lvov-Sandomierz operation. These riflemen were probably 'tank-riders' on the T-34 Model 1943 tank nearby, a common Soviet tactic owing to the lack of armoured infantry vehicles.

A T-34 Model 1943 tank of the 1st Byelorussian Front supported by infantry advances past the burning wrecks of two German PzKpfw IV tanks during the Lvov-Sandomierz operation. (Sovfoto)

Many of the worst atrocities committed in Warsaw were carried out by German units recruited from ex-Russian prisoners-of-war. The Kaminsky brigade, spurred on by their rabidly anti-Polish commander, was active throughout Operation Bagration. It spearheaded the anti-partisan sweeps behind the German Third Panzer and Fourth armies, of which Kormoran was the third since April 1944. Fresh from the massacres between Lepel and Borisov, the 6000 strong brigade was dispatched to Warsaw where Kaminsky's activities so disgusted the SS that they murdered him in turn, his death faked as a Polish ambush.

Despite the reign of terror perpetrated by the SS and Wehrmacht security detachments, the Russian partisans severely disrupted the German rail

A river barge brings two Soviet T-34 Model 1943 tanks over the Vistula to reinforce the Sandomierz bridgehead. The barge is being towed by two Soviet BMK-70 motor boats, a standard Soviet engineer craft used for river-crossing operations. (Sovfoto)

net. Their raids are ideal subjects for tactical wargames of any format; boardgames, miniatures or role-play. Co-ordinated from Moscow and supported by aerial supply drops, the partisans operated in company and battalion strength, sometimes combining for major raids, but usually remaining dispersed to avoid offering the Germans a concentrated target. The Germans lacked the manpower to garrison every cross-roads or guard every stretch of rail track. Instead, they occupied strongpoints along key routes, intended to be able to hold off the lightly-armed partisans until help could arrive. Companies of motorised infantry stood ready to race to the rescue when a strongpoint was attacked, but bad weather, partisan ambushes or Soviet air strikes could delay them long enough for the garrison to be overwhelmed.

Large forests and the forbidding Ushachi swamp provided the partisans with so many hiding places that entire communities, let alone weapons caches could be concealed from the Germans. Anti-partisan operations were near the bottom of the Luftwaffe's priorities and the Germans could only expect air support during major 'search and destroy' operations like Kormoran or Frühlingsfest. Whether you design your own rules or favour *Advanced Squad Leader* or one of the many sets of published miniatures rules, these desperate little battles make excellent wargames. They are more typical of the Eastern Front experience than the massed tank armies of Kursk, and if you construct your scenarios with care, you can complete them in an evening. They are also an antidote to the sort of micro-tank games in which the German forces seem to consist entirely of Tigers and Panthers. German security forces often used captured enemy equipment like obsolete French tanks; as noted above, the best of the German armour was in Army Group North Ukraine, and even the frontline divisions of Army Group Centre relied on assault guns for armoured support.

Marxist military doctrine emphasises the 'correlation of forces': comparing the military and political strengths of rival armies and states. By any analysis, Army Group Centre was doomed from the moment Operation Bagration was launched. Even if Hitler had consented to a timely retreat to the 'Tiger Line' or beyond, neither Manstein nor Model could have defeated the Soviet offensive by the sort of deft counterstroke delivered in the past. The odds were too unfavourable and the German army no longer had the same qualitative advantage that it had once enjoyed. So the

Germans were doomed to retreat. Withdrawal in the face of an active enemy is one of the most difficult of all military operations. (Moltke the elder, on being praised for his genius by a sycophantic officer, observed that he could lay no such claim as he had never had to conduct a retreat.) Hitler's 'no retreat' orders and the excellent leadership of many Soviet tank formations left over 100,000 German soldiers surrounded. There were major encirclements at Vitebsk, Minsk, Bobruisk, Vilnius and Brest, while the pace of the Russian advance created many smaller 'pockets'.

Since the annihilation of the Korsun pocket during the winter offensive, which earned the ruthless Koniev his promotion to Marshal, German soldiers knew the grim fate awaiting them. On occasion the Russians killed captured German prisoners, but many more died in the hands of the NKVD when force marched to POW camps or in the camps themselves from disease or malnutrition. The Russians' behaviour might seem inexcusable, but near Minsk they did capture several trains packed with Russian children awaiting deportation. The Germans habitually massacred villagers or took them back to the Reich for use as slave labour. And yet the retreating German soldiers were often accompanied by Russian civilians equally anxious to escape the Red Army. Minsk had been occupied since 1941 and many people had made their peace with the occupying power — and the NKVD neither forgave nor forgot.

Since German forces are going to be fleeing west, a 'retreat game' is probably the best way to recreate the destruction of Army Group Centre on a tabletop. German battalions were so depleted that a small battlegroup can be assembled on a scale as low as one figure/three soldiers. Thirty figures can represent a battalion, with a far higher proportion of MG42s and mortars than normal, since the heavy weapons were retained as long as possible. Together with a Pak 40 or two, a couple of half-tracks, some lorries, a few horse-drawn wagons and (if you are lucky) a tank, they form

To reinforce the Vistula river bridgeheads, the Soviets commandeered river barges. Here T-34 Model 1943 tanks of the Polish 1st Tank Brigade prepare to cross the Vistula river to reinforce the Magnuszew bridgehead. To help save space on the barge, the unit's jeep has been manhandled onto the engine deck of one of the tanks. (Janusz Magnuski)

the core of a beleaguered unit trying to fight its way back to German lines. I use a 'road movie' style game in which you travel down the length of a wargames table, encountering randomised Russian forces at the capricious turn of a playing card. This suits any number of players; it works as a solo game, or with several players all on the German side, fighting Red Army units that are controlled by cards and dice. It can work equally well with Russian player(s), split between regular army and partisans. There are several manufacturers producing suitable metal figures in 20mm scale as well as 15mm and 1/200. GHQ's incredible range of 1/285 micro armour needs no introduction. However, the most cost-effective option is to use the splendid range of 1/72 plastic figures produced by Revell; this includes German and Russian infantry plus a very useful pack of German engineers. The latter provides a handful of characters lobbing anti-tank mines, just the sort of lantern-jawed veterans to tackle a wave of T-34s.

I use cards to trigger random events and Russian activity, while dice rolls determine the progress of the little column down the table. I roll 3 D6 for vehicles, moving them the score in inches. Non-cross country vehicles travel at half speed off road and bog down if any '1's are rolled; half-tracks or armoured cars bog on two '1's; tanks need to roll three '1's together to get stuck. Random events include Russian airstrikes, from a regiment of Il-2s to single Po-2 biplane, partisan attacks and re-supply by Ju-52. Incidentally, a German airdrop increases the chance of a Russian attack and the parachuted supplies are not always what is required; possible contents including ammunition of the wrong calibre for your anti-tank gun, fleapowder and signed photographs of the Führer. I use a similar system for a role-play game, and woe betide any player who fails to greet the latter like a good national socialist. He or she might survive to reach German lines, only to be demoted to a penal battalion. After all, the German army only survived on the Eastern Front by the application of ferocious discipline. In two months at Stalingrad, the German Sixth army executed more of its own men than the British Army did in the four years 1914-18. For a first hand account of what it was like to retreat through Russia, see Guy Sajer's *The Forgotten Soldier*, recently re-published by Brasseys.

The cards enable the column to receive reinforcements, ranging from a handful of other survivors to a tank or half-track unit. But red picture cards always bring trouble, ultimately the great wave of T-34s and lend-lease M4 Shermans that rolls across the table, riflemen perched on top. Serried ranks of figures follow in its wake. With luck, you might be able to dig in first, before the hail of katyusha rockets and the creeping barrage. The Russian infantry can be separated from their tanks if you open fire with the Pak 40s and MG42s at long range, but this exposes your positions to tank gunfire. Eventually the tanks crash over your forward trenches, some possibly being destroyed by a panzerfaust or anti-tank mine. If there is no Russian player, I dice for the movement of the T-34s, making them increasingly likely to fire from the short halt as they close on the German position. If the German player's luck holds, the Russians may not spot the German gun positions until too late, and they may attack the wrong part of your line. But then, 1944 was not a lucky year for the German army.